The Gendered Pulpit:

Sex, Body, and Desire in Preaching and Worship

Angela M. Yarber

The Gendered Pulpit:
Sex, Body, and Desire in Preaching and Worship

Angela M. Yarber

Parson's Porch Books

The Gendered Pulpit: Sex, Body and Desire in Preaching and Worship

ISBN: Softcover 978-1-936912-66-7

Graphic Design on Cover by MaryBeth Byram

Photograph on Cover by Greg Ledbetter

To order additional copies of this book, contact:

Parson's Porch Books
1-423-475-7308
www.parsonsporchbooks.com

Parsons Porch Books is an imprint of Parson's Porch & Company (PP&C) in Cleveland, Tennessee. PP&C is an innovative non-profit organization which raises money by publishing books of noted authors, representing all genres. All donations from contributors and profits from publishing are shared with the poor.

Dedicated to
Elizabeth, always

Table of Contents

Acknowledgments

GENDERING THE PULPIT IS NOT TYPICALLY SOMETHING one can do alone. Rather, there are many people to thank along the way. Foremost, I am grateful for Rev. Dr. David Russell Tullock and the work of Parson's Porch & Company with its publishing services. Your mission is admirable, your work prophetic. I am honored to write with you. Gendering the pulpit also typically occurs within the confines of faith communities. So, I am thankful for four faith communities who have stood with me in this process, allowing me time and space in their pulpits: the Oaks Baptist Church, Parkway Baptist Church, Shell Ridge Community Church, and Wake Forest Baptist Church. It has been an honor to call myself your pastor at various times over the past thirteen years.

Then there are those myriad voices we never hear. For those countless women and LGBTQ persons who have lifted your voices in bold proclamations, but who have not had the privilege of an official pulpit, thank you. This book is for you. And for all those women and LGBTQ persons who don't think that preaching could be a part of your future, it is my hope that this book will tell you otherwise. Know that you are beloved, affirmed, worthwhile, and called; do not let anyone tell you differently. Raise you voice. Affirm your body, for it is holy.

My dear friends, family, and colleagues are foremost among those I wish to acknowledge. Wendy, Melissa, Ryan, Amy, Richard, Jen, Sharon, Trisha, Patricia, MaryBeth, Jill, Michelle, Diane, Andrea, Ron, Weave, Susan, mom, dad, Carl, Josh, and many others continue to be a support system filled with good humor and prophetic challenge. Thank you. And for Elizabeth, who listens to endless processing, proofreads countless documents, and makes me laugh every day, I am thankful. You make me a better person and gendering the pulpit in the direction of justice would be no fun without you. I remain hopeful for our future Tango and how we will make the world a better place together.

Chapter 1

Introductions

On a sunny Sunday morning in California, I was talking with my congregants following worship. I made it a point to find nine-year-old Jake because he had helped lead in worship that morning. I wanted to thank him and tell him that he did a good job. As I spoke with him, his five-year-old sister, Emma, stood behind him with her little head down, peeking out from behind her hair to glance up at her then twenty-something pastor.

"Hello, Emma," I said, knowing that she wouldn't respond. Emma didn't really talk to grown-ups, even if they were only twenty-something. "She's embarrassed," Jake informed me. "Embarrassed? Why?" I asked her brother, confused. "Because at home she dresses up and pretends to be you, dancing around the house and preaching. She even wears a scarf and pretends it's one of those things," he said, pointing to my stole. Emma's grandmother approached and added another detail to the story. "Sometimes she serves communion to her stuffed animals and then performs a dance," Grandma Betty informed me. Emma blushed and smiled. I squatted down to look in her little eyes and said, "Keep dancing, Emma; you can be anything you want to be."

Needless to say, I was flattered. But flattery does not capture the essence of Emma's emulation. Instead, I think back on Emma, now approaching her teens, and the other little girls in that congregation. I think about their perception of what it means to be a preacher. For Emma, her vision of a preacher is a young woman. When she receives communion, it is a lesbian who holds the bread and proclaims, "The body of Christ, broken for you." And when someone asks Emma what a professional dancer looks like, she describes her healthy minister who dances in worship and while preaching. If someone were to tell Emma that women or LGBTQ persons are not called to preach, she would have no idea what they are talking about. So, I begin a book about gendering the pulpit with the story of a five-year-old girl dressing up and pretending to be her preacher, dancing, proclaiming the Word, and serving communion to her stuffed animals.

I do so because for centuries the pulpit has been gendered in particular ways, namely straight and male. Those afforded the privileges of ordination, those whose bodies mattered, were valuable enough to step into the pulpit, affirmed enough to proclaim. Over time, things have begun to shift, though we still have a long way to go before every pulpit is gendered in the direction of justice, inclusion, and radical hospitality. Since I firmly believe in the notion, "if you can't see it, you can't be it," I have devoted all of my adulthood to shifting the status quo when it comes to preaching and worship, doing my best to gender the pulpit in a manner that creates pathways for women and LGBTQ persons to see that they, too, can be called to proclaim the Word. When I step into the pulpit each Sunday, I do so on behalf of countless people who never dreamed that they were affirmed and beloved of God, let alone that they, too, have a Word to share. So, I write these words about how preaching and worship intersect with sex, gender, sexuality, the body, dance, and disorder on their behalf. As we explore these myriad avenues for gendering the pulpit, two questions undergird our discussion. How does the body gender the pulpit? How does the sermon construct the body?

In order to respond to these questions, I find it first imperative to define a couple of key terms that will be used throughout this book. Since the first part of this book deals primarily with the role of sex in preaching and worship, it is important to define the acronym LGBTQ. This acronym—while not exhaustive—refers to the lesbian, gay, bisexual, transgender, questioning, and queer community. It is an affirmative label from within the community that attempts to name some of the particularities otherwise excluded by terms such as gay or homosexual. Some extend the acronym to include LGBTIQA to intentionally name those who are intersex or allies. There is no doubt that the LGBTQ community has been and continues to be excluded from preaching ministry in many denominations and local churches. As an ordained lesbian Baptist preacher, I find it important to highlight these marginalized voices in the pages that follow.

Also in need of defining is a word included in the above acronym, a word that often results in heated conversation both inside and outside of the LGBTQ community. This word is queer. Some LGBTQ individuals—especially from older generations—may recoil at this term because it has been used in a pejorative and malicious way in the past. In the same way that other oppressed and marginalized groups have reclaimed terms once deemed derogatory and translated them to have an empowering and redemptive meaning, so too have many in the LGBTQ community. It's important in this discussion to remember that the meanings of words evolve over time; some words that were once acceptable are now inappropriate, offensive, or politically incorrect and visa versa.

Queer can be understood in three primary ways, all of which are evoked throughout this book. The first is as an umbrella term for the LGBTIQA community. Referring to lesbian, gay, bisexual, transgender, intersex, questioning, and allied people as "queer" is a way of including everyone without resorting to what some have called an "alphabet soup acronym." Referring to all these different types of people as "queer" is also a way of including both sexual orientation and gender identity. A second understanding of queer harkens back to its original definition, which is "strange, odd, peculiar, eccentric, or transgressive." In this manner, "queer" becomes a self-conscious embrace of those intentionally transgressing societal norms with regard to sexual orientation and gender identity. To "queer" something is to disrupt the status quo and upset convention. The third and final way of defining queer is as a way of erasing boundaries. This understanding is grounded in the academic discipline of queer theory, which arose in the early 1990s. Queer theory seeks to deconstruct societal boundaries regarding sexuality and gender. Queer theorists maintain that the traditional binary categories of gender and sexuality are actually social constructions rather than biological essences. So, someone is queer if that individual deconstructs socially constructed elements of gender or sexuality.

When I use the term queer in the pages that follow, I do so in a way that encompasses all three of these understandings. What is more, I would contend that the call of the preacher, the good news we are to proclaim, is itself queer in that it is transgressive, it upsets the status quo, and it liberates the oppressed and marginalized. When I speak of gendering the pulpit in the direction of justice, I also evoke the notion of queering the pulpit so that it includes the voices of those who have been ignored or silenced. When we examine the bodies that Jesus preached to—
whom Jesus included in his ministry—we realize that his efforts were quite queer. He turned all kinds of societal norms upside down and upset the status quo on myriad occasions. To gender the pulpit in the direction of justice—in the direction of Jesus—I would contend that one simply must be a bit queer.

The Gendered Pulpit is divided into two parts, with each part containing two chapters. Part I deals with sex and the gendered pulpit. The chapters within Part I specifically address gender and sexuality in preaching and worship. Building off of Part I, Part II deals with the body and the gendered pulpit. The chapters within Part II address the body affirmed and the body gone awry. Here, I claim that the body is affirmed by dance and the body goes awry with eating disorders. Each chapter is structured in the same way. The entry point into each topic—gender, sexuality, dance, and disorder—is personal narrative. I find that sharing a story stemming from my experience as a lesbian woman preacher who has both danced professionally and recovered from eating disorders makes theoretical conversations more accessible and relatable. The theoretical is what follows the personal narrative in each chapter. This section, too, shares the same structure in each chapter. Accordingly, I address each topic in scripture, history, theology, and in theories of preaching and worship. These subsections are intended to be illustrative rather than exhaustive; an entire book could be dedicated to each section. It is my aim to offer glimpses into theories that may help the preacher gender the pulpit. Finally, each chapter concludes with two practical applications of the chapter's topic. The practical applications include liturgical elements, such as prayers, music, and liturgies, and a sermon. It is my hope that the practical applications can serve as tools or methods for implementing the theoretical.

The questions posed here and in each chapter are intended to be open-ended. Rather than providing clear-cut answers, I offer responses that evoke further quandary and action on behalf of those seeking to gender the pulpit in the direction of justice. How does the body gender the pulpit? How does the sermon construct the body? Let's find out…

Part I
Chapter 2

Sex and the Gendered Pulpit

"YOU DON'T LOOK LIKE A PREACHER." I cannot tell you the number of times I have heard this after answering the age-old question upon meeting someone new: "What do you do for a living?" From astonishment to wonder to downright fury, countless individuals have responded with the same six words: "You don't look like a preacher." This is typically the response upon looking at a young woman. Just wait until they discover that I'm also a lesbian. Then all hell breaks loose!

What it "looks like" to be a preacher, clergy, or worship-leader is something that the church and society has tenuously constructed over time. Straight, male, and often celibate is what is understood, accepted, normative. But what about those who exist outside of this norm, namely women and the LGBTQ community? What role does sex have in preaching and worship? Does sex make the preaching event different, unique, subversive? If so, how?

How does the act of preaching construct gender and sexuality? How does sex construct the sermon? What does it mean for the gendered and sexualized body to step into the pulpit? Part I of *The Gendered Pulpit* seeks to respond to these questions by exploring personal experience, scripture, history, theology, theories in preaching and worship, and practical applications that deal with the issue of sex. Sex is typically understood to encompass both gender and sexuality, so each of these elements comprises a chapter within the first part of this book. Before elaborating on the structure that will follow in both of these chapters, I find it imperative to define this complex notion of sex through the concept of positionality.

Defining sex is no easy thing. I'm not speaking of the sex act, but of the overlapping issues of gender and sexuality. Since the particularity of one's sex has prohibited countless women and LGBTQ persons from the possibilities of preaching or ordained ministry for centuries, expounding further on the subject is worthwhile. A brief warning: we're about to delve into feminist and queer theory. While it appears heady on the surface, these revolutionary theories have been the stepping stones by which women and LGBTQ persons have actually made their way into the pulpit. So, we owe it to these theorists to open our minds and listen. The mind is, indeed, a part of the gendered and sexualized body, after all.

As the history of feminist theory illustrates, defining woman is not as simple as merely referencing someone born biologically with female genitalia or XX chromosomes. Rather, beginning with such monumental work as Simone de Beauvoir, scholars have struggled with how to name "woman" in reference to gender, sexuality, race, ethnicity, and class. Primary is the acknowledgement that the way in which gender is constructed and understood is not universal, but varies widely from culture to culture and age to age. In my perspective, an introductory glimpse into the Essentialist versus Constructivist debate will prove helpful in discussing how to gender the pulpit in the direction of justice, equality, and radical hospitality.

Feminist philosopher, Linda Alcoff, details an informative and accessible survey of the abovementioned debate in her article "Cultural Feminism versus Post-Structuralism: The Identity Crisis in Feminist Theory."[1] Many of the forerunners in feminist theory found themselves in the Cultural Feminist or Essentialist camp. Examples include Mary Daly or Adrienne Rich. Such essentialists, or cultural feminists, assert that there is an underlying essence of what it means to be woman; this essence must be valued and revalidated in the midst of patriarchy

---

[1]Linda Alcoff, "Cultural Feminism versus Post-Structuralism: The Identity Crisis in Feminist Theory," in *Feminist Theory: A Reader*, ed. Wendy Kolmar and Frances Bartkowski (New York: McGraw Hill, 2005): 426-436.

and misogyny. It is worthwhile to keep in mind that these essentialists were forerunners fighting against those who equated "feminine" attributes with depravity, or reasons for withholding rights and responsibilities from women. For this reason, essentialists highlight seemingly "feminine" attributes—sensitivity, emotion, nurture, care, and an overarching "female consciousness"[2]—that guides what it means to be a woman, regardless of culture, religion, class, ethnicity, race, or orientation. These female virtues, according to the essentialists, stem from women's distinct biology as intrinsically different and oppositional to men's biology. It's worth noting that Alcoff claims that she is hard-pressed to find women from oppressed nationalities and races in the category of cultural feminism.[3] While some feminist scholars may argue that Cherríe Moraga or Audre Lorde have essentialist tendencies, the role of cultural identity, oppression because of race, ethnicity, class, or sexual identity often preclude many marginalized women from ascribing to an essentialist "we're-all-in-this-together" mentality that sometimes ignores other forms of oppression.

On the other end of the feminist spectrum are the constructivists. Alcoff calls these constructivists the post-structuralists. The aim of feminist constructivists and post-structuralists is to deconstruct the concept of any subject having an essential identity. So, constructivists reject biological determinism by asserting that humans are actually over-determined, or constructed, by society. What an essentialist sees as a biological essence, a constructivist sees as something society has constructed, created, and inscribed onto one's identity. In this manner, "woman" is a social construct developed and created over time; it is not the essence of one's innate being or determined by one's genitalia. So, her sex could be female, but her gender does not necessarily have to be woman. It is here that the work of queer theorist Judith Butler is most helpful. Butler

---

[2] "Female consciousness" is a phrase coined by Adrienne Rich to encompass these virtues. For more information, see Adrienne Rich, *On Lies, Secrets, and Silence* (New York: Norton, 1979), 18.
[3] Alcoff, 428.

notes the way in which philosophers "rarely think about acting in the theatrical sense, but they do have a discourse of 'acts' that maintains associative semantic meanings with theories of performance and acting…[gender] is an identity tenuously constituted in time—an identity instituted through a *stylized repetition of acts*."[4] A woman's acts determine her gender identity, not her biology or the label given to her by society, according to constructivists.

Further, Butler and other queer theorists would add that society has constructed a constraining set of binaries that place unfair limitations on sex. The most obvious binaries include male/female, men/women, and gay/straight. These binaries function in opposition to one another. Queer theorists challenge us to see what exists in the interstitial space between the binaries, or even better, if we dismantle the binaries altogether. Dualistic binaries inevitably create hierarchies as one binary is elevated at the expense of the other. In society in general, and in preaching in particular, we see most often that the male is elevated as superior and ordainable, while the female is dismissed as subservient and unordainable. Similarly, the straight preacher finds a pulpit, while the LGBTQ preacher is left searching for a place of proclamation based solely on having a sexualized identity that is discriminated against and devalued. One only need look at official church doctrine or polity to see both of these hierarchical binaries explicitly and implicitly played out in the direction of patriarchy and heterosexism. If you desire to look further, simply walk into the average church in the average town and see who stands behind the pulpit each Sunday.

The theoretic discourse of both essentialists and constructivists may seem dense or inapplicable to everyday life or preaching and worship at first glance. As theory-bound and seemingly esoteric as it may be, acknowledging the deep complexities of gender and sexuality is vital in understanding how we might gender the pulpit in the direction of justice. I find that Alcoff's compromise between essentialism and

---

[4] Judith Butler, "Performative Acts and Gender Constitution: An Essay in Phenomenology and Feminist Theory," *Theatre Journal* 49:1 (December 1988): 401-402. Italics mine.

constructivism is a beneficial approach. Calling her approach "positionality," she states poignantly her middle-ground: "When the concept of 'woman' is defined not by a particular set of attributes but by a particular *position*, the internal characteristics of the person thus identified are not denoted so much as they are external context within which that person is situated."[5] Like Alcoff, I find the notion of positionality applicable to the idea of gendering the pulpit. The sermon, the pulpit, and worship do have biological essences, so they should not be understood to be innately male or female (or limited to either of these binaries). Over time, however, Christians have certainly constructed a socially understood norm when it comes to preaching, worship, and who has the power and privilege of presiding at such holy responsibilities. How might we position the pulpit differently? How might the positionality of the pulpit subvert these oppressive constructions and, instead, create holy spaces for women and LGBTQ persons to proclaim the word?

In Part I of this book I explore these intersecting questions in two related chapters. Chapter three is about gender and chapter four is about sexuality. Each chapter is divided into three major sections: personal experience, theory, and practical application. The theoretical sections include examples in scripture, church history, theology, and theories in preaching and worship. These subsections are not intended to be exhaustive, but illustrative of the wider issues and how these issues intersect with preaching and worship. It is my hope that the combination of personal experience, theory, and practical application will provide readers with tangible tools for gendering the pulpit toward justice.

---

[5] Alcoff, 435.

Chapter 3

The Gendered Body: Preaching, Worship, and Gender

A NUMBER OF FANTASTIC FEMINIST SCHOLARS have dedicated their lives and research to the role of gender in Christianity and ministry: Mary Daly, Rosemary Radford Ruether, Letty Russell, Elisabeth Schüssler Fiorenza, Elizabeth Johnson, Catherine Keller, Marcella Althaus-Reid, Karen Baker-Fletcher, Chung Hyun Kyung, and Ada Maria Isasi-Diaz just to name a few. So, too, have women in preaching: Barbara Brown Taylor, Mary Donovan Turner, Teresa Fry Brown, Mary Lin Hudson, Christine Smith, Linda Clader, Jana Childers, Anna Carter Florence, and many others. These brave and prophetic women stand on the shoulders of women whose "testimonies" gave voice to the patriarchal systems that otherwise rendered them mute throughout the ages: Anna Julia Cooper, Jerena Lee, Sarah Osborn, Anne Marbury Hutchinson, Sojourner Truth, Hildegard of Bingen, Catherine of Siena, Louisa Mariah Layman Woosley, Julian of Norwich, Beverly Wildung Harrison, and all the other women whose names and stories we do not know, but who surely raised their voices in hearty proclamation over the centuries. These women have gendered the pulpit throughout Christendom and their stories—whether explicitly mentioned or not—are the foundations upon which this chapter stands.

This chapter asks, "How does the act of preaching construct gender and how does gender construct the sermon?" In order to answer these questions I open with a story from personal experience. Then I examine the role of gender in scripture, church history, theology, and preaching and worship in particular. After a personal story and an examination of scripture, history, and theology, I provide two practical ways for preachers to address the gendered body in preaching and worship. Let us begin in my tenth year of ministry when I was twenty-eight years old…

Little Girls in Ministry

I met a friend and colleague one day in her office at the seminary where she is a professor. We were going to lunch. On our way out of the office, we ran into the new president of the seminary in the hallway. My friend introduced us. "This is Angela Yarber," she told the new president. "She's an associate pastor at my church. She was ordained years ago. She's nearly finished with her Ph.D. She has taught classes at the seminary in the past…" She continued to rattle off my credentials as though she was reading the new president my curriculum vitae. I was confused as to why she was doing this, but I stood there smiling politely until she finished.

The new president looked me up and down from toe to head. He was much taller and older than me and his size seemed to shrink and diminish my small 5'5" frame. "But you're such a little girl," he said surprised. My friend began again to list accomplishments. "I suppose I'm older than I look," I said jokingly to him. I extended my hand to offer a hearty handshake and told him that it was a pleasure meeting him. As we walked away, he hollered, "Bye bye little girl!" My friend whipped around and said, "I'm not sure if you heard me, but [insert my list of credentials once again]…Maybe you should be saying, 'bye bye strong woman!'"
He laughed.

I was somewhat taken aback by her strong words. I'm accustomed to people assuming I'm younger than I am, or that I lack experience, and I delight in proving them otherwise. My friend and colleague, who is always my advocate, reminded me that I should be just as horrified when someone belittles me as I would be if that same person belittled one of my friends. I would have been furious if the president of a seminary—someone who should know better—called one of my colleagues a "little girl." At the time I was a professor and a pastor with over ten years of experience and qualifications. I am not a little girl.

"Imagine if you were a man in his late twenties," my friend said to me. "He wouldn't dare say, 'bye bye little boy' to a male colleague!"

The same president came to my church as a guest preacher nearly a year later. Since he's the president of a Baptist seminary, we thought it wise to invite him into our pulpit. I'd recently finished my doctorate and was dancing in worship that day. Barefoot, small, and clad in a bright red dance dress for Pentecost, I once again extended by hand to this president for a hearty shake. I broadened by shoulders and looked him square in the eyes. "Welcome to our church; we're glad to have you here. I'm not sure if you remember me, but I'm the associate pastors here," I said, trying to sound professional in my bare feet and red dress.

"Hello little girl. You're so young and little. I can't believe you're a pastor," he responded.

I asked around to make sure that my internal response wasn't overly dramatic and every one of my male and female colleagues were much angrier than I was at his words. Maybe it's an age thing. Maybe it's something cultural that I've missed. I don't think he's a bad guy or egregiously sexist. He's not some ignoramus off the street who thinks women should only bear children and bake pies. He's the president of a *progressive* seminary. And a president of a seminary should know better. I don't say these words to indict him as a person, but to draw attention to abuses of power and divisions of privilege. Never would a grown man refer to another grown man as a "little boy" if he were his colleague. Yet, because I am a young woman—with just as many credentials as him—I am a "little girl."

So, "little girls," listen up! You may make seventy cents for every dollar a man makes. You may have to work twice as hard to be recognized for half as much. You may be called "little" or "young" or "pretty" or "cute" rather than "strong" or "powerful" or "smart" or "accomplished." But you are just as strong, powerful, smart, and accomplished as any man. And together we're going to work our hardest to change the flawed and patriarchal system that tells you otherwise. Together, we're going to gender the pulpit.

Scripture and the Gendered Pulpit

There are countless ways a preacher could approach scripture in terms of gender and feminism. Utilizing a hermeneutic of suspicion, where the preacher exegetes the text with the awareness of the prevalence of patriarchy embedded in the context, writing, editing, canonizing, translating, and interpreting of scripture, is imperative. The works of key feminist biblical scholars, such as Phylis Trible, Elisabeth Schüssler Fiorenza, and Athalaya Brenner highlight these approaches. Similarly, a feminist can also "exorcise" the demons in the text by rejecting and overturning those elements of scripture that are dehumanizing, oppressive, and sexist; Mary Daly outlines such an approach in her seminal text, *The Church and the Second Sex*.[6] Another approach is to uncover the often overlooked roles of women in scripture and elevate the power of the female voice in prophecy, justice, and in relation to Jesus and the formation of the early church. Wonderful feminist scholars have also done this important work. Since so much of what preachers and liturgists do emphasizes the power of language, I'd like to examine five key terms found in scripture and illuminate how these "feminine" terms have the potential to gender the pulpit in a manner that promotes equality, justice, and empowerment. These words are *ruah*, *hokhma*, *sophia*, *el shaddai*, and *shekhina*.

The Hebrew word *ruah* is a feminine word for spirit, wind, or breath. *Ruah ha kodesh* is literally the Holy Spirit, or the spirit of YHWH. She was present at the creation of the world in Genesis, perhaps a part of the "us" in the creation narrative when the biblical writer states that God proclaimed "let *us* make humankind in *our* image." Co-creating alongside of YHWH, she breathed life into humankind. Early Jews, and even early Christians, thought of her as the breath of life, a vital force that dwelled within the human body. *Ruah* is the divine breath

---

[6] See chapter five in Mary Daly, *The Church and the Second Sex* (Boston: Beacon Press, 1968).

that fills humans and the moment she leaves a human, that human dies. This spirit or breath enlivens prophecy and wisdom in God's people and is unequivocally feminine in nature. According to Elizabeth Johnson, *ruah's* activities include: "creating new life, working to sustain it in myriad ways, renewing what has been damaged, grieving over destruction, teaching people to be wise, and inspiring critique and enthusiasm, all of which have engaged the energies of generation after generation of women."[7] The spirit, therefore, when thought of by early Jews and Christians was invariably female, referred to as "she."

Another important gendered word in scripture is *hokhma*. *Hokhma* is the feminine noun for wisdom used throughout the Hebrew bible. She is featured throughout the entire corpus of Jewish wisdom literature, including Proverbs, Job, and Ecclesiastes. You can find *hokhma* 149 times in the Hebrew bible. And because the spirit of God—*ruah*—was understood by Jews to be the voice of God, revealing God's thoughts and desires, the spirit was closely linked with God's wisdom, *hokhma*.[8] This "Spirit of Wisdom," also invariably feminine, guides those whose very hearts beat with the divine pathos of God, the prophets, which call the people to justice, kindness, and humility. Because these prophets are filled with the spirit of God, they may act with the wisdom of God. Both spirit and wisdom are gendered feminine in nature. Such is also true in the Greek form of wisdom.

Sophia is the Greek feminine word for wisdom in the New Testament. Her characteristics are similar to the Hebrew *hokhma*, but expand in early Christian theology as she is understood as a divine attribute, or part of the trinity. In these ways, *sophia* is portrayed as a hypostasis of God's wisdom, or a part of God's substance. Accordingly, early trinitarian formulas reference God the father, Jesus the son, and Sophia the spirit. A female spirit was undeniably an early part of the trinity. This is illustrated most poignantly in a Gnostic text, the Gospel of Philip, which states, "Some say, 'Mary conceived by the Holy

---

[7] Elizabeth Johnson, *She Who Is* (New York: Crossroad, 1992), 83.
[8] April DeConick, *Holy Misogyny* (New York: Continuum, 2011), 4.

Spirit.' They are wrong. They do not know what they are saying. When did a woman ever become pregnant by a woman?"[9]

It is worth noting that such an early understanding of the trinity, and of an unequivocally feminine spirit, was once normative. The Spirit was understood as and spoken of as a "she." April DeConick highlights the difficulty of such an understanding today: "[W]hat must be realized is that Judaism and Christianity are the products of centuries of religious developments. So what might have been considered 'orthodox' at an early time, a few centuries later might be considered 'heretical' because the tradition and practices had drastically changed by then."[10] What was once orthodox—a female *sophia* spirit—has slowly yet intentionally been overshadowed by patriarchal understandings of the trinity and the spirit in such a way that calling the spirit a "she" is cause for giggles at best and outrage at worst.

I recall once attending an academic conference where Molly Marshall was receiving an award after the recent publication of her book on pneumatology, *Joining the Dance: A Theology of the Spirit*.[11] When accepting the award, Marshall casually, yet prophetically gendered the pulpit/podium when she referenced the spirit, saying, "bless *her*." Nervous male laughter tittered throughout the room. I looked around and noticed that Marshall and I were some of the only women present. What was once seen as orthodox—a female *sophia* wisdom—is now most often understood as male. The pulpit is gendered, however, the moment we stop our giggles and allow *sophia's* wisdom to become a part of our beings, words, voices.

Yet another gendered word found in scripture is a Hebrew title for God, *el shaddai.* Traditionally translated as God Almighty, *el shaddai* is laden with debate over the meaning of *shaddai*. *El* is always understood in Hebrew, Ugarit, and Canaanite as "god." *Shaddai*, however, is more complicated.

[9] *Gospel of Philip* 55:23-26.

[10] DeConick, 7.

[11] Molly Marshall, *Joining the Dance* (Valley Forge: Judson Press, 2003).

Some scholars assert that it translates as "God of the mountains." This could be a reference to Mount Sinai where God gave Moses the Ten Commandments, along with a myriad other mountainous references in the Hebrew bible. It could also refer to the Mesopotamian divine mountain. Other scholars claim that *shaddai* stems from the Hebrew *šad* or *shadayim*, meaning "breast" or "breasts." Some of these scholars also relate *shaddai* to the Semetic goddess. In both cases, *el shaddai* translates as "the breasted one" or "the one of the breast." Many ancient Jews also referred to particular mountains and mountain ranges with female names because they looked similar to the curves or breasts of women or goddesses. In these ways, "the breasted one" and the "God of the mountains" are actually synonymous. A God of the mountains is also a God of breasts, or a breasted one.

A final gendered word is *shekhina*. *Shekhina* literally translates as "dwelling" or "settling," but its connotation refers to God's presence on earth. Like every other word discussed, it is also feminine. She was originally understood to dwell within the most inner sanctuary of the Temple, the Holy of Holies, but with the second destruction of the Temple in 70 CE, she was left to dwell outside its walls. Like the Israelites, she wanders in exile, filling God's people with her presence as a form of comfort and love. In Jewish writings, she was a synonym for God's presence among the people.[12] Her spirit enlivens us still today.

There is no question that scripture is riddled with misogyny. Patriarchal writers, redactors, and interpreters have maligned women's voices in scripture for ages. But gendering the pulpit does not involve disregarding scripture altogether. In fact, we remain most faithful to the text when we understand its historical contexts, translate it in its original languages, and do our best to understand its original intentions. As we have seen, hidden in the crevices of the canon are gendered words that have the potential for empowering and inspiring women's voices and lives. *Ruah*, *hokhma*, *sophia*, *el shaddai*, and *shekhina* are not simply feminine words in Hebrew or Greek. They are words that encapsulate the very spirit, wisdom, and presence of God.

[12] Johnson, 85.

Proclaiming these feminine words is an important part of gendering the pulpit. Nevertheless, scripture has been used as a bludgeon throughout history as verses are plucked from their context and used to oppress and marginalize countless groups of people. Primary to this project is the role of women and the LGBTQ community in history. Since the next chapter is dedicated to sexuality, here I will address our gendered history by focusing on its particular role in the Baptist denomination.

History and the Gendered Pulpit

When discussing how the pulpit helps construct gender and how gender helps construct the sermon historically, one could look at the history of women's ordination throughout all denominations. I considered this possibility and determined that it would be more helpful to narrow the focus to one particular denomination. And since personal narratives are often my starting point, I decided that a brief history of my own personal denomination would prove fruitful. I have found that Baptists and Catholics seem to receive the most heat when it comes to gendered roles in the church. Ironically, I am an ordained Baptist minister and my female partner is Catholic. It is true that Roman Catholics and *Southern* Baptists do not permit women to be ordained, while about half of all Protestant denominations do ordain women; it is also true that only about 15% of all ordained clergy in the U.S. are female.[13]

Because of the key Baptist principles of local church autonomy, freedom of conscience, and the priesthood of all believers, Baptist stances on women and gender are as varied as the people and churches that constitute the broad denomination. The Baptist World Alliance hosts over two hundred Baptist groups, while one of the largest groupings of Baptists—the Southern Baptist Convention—chooses not to affiliate with BWA because of how "liberal" their network can be. Sects within the denomination, and individuals within those sects, are as far left as the Alliance of Baptists (an open and affirming Baptist movement) or as far right as Southern Baptists. Still

---

[13] http://www.bls.gove/cps/wlf-databook2006.htm.

much of the controversy over the gendered pulpit centers around the Southern Baptist Convention.

The Southern Baptist Convention (SBC) was formed in 1845 and "messengers" were sent from individual churches to vote on matters that impacted the denomination at an annual conference. In 1885 women were refused admission to the annual meeting and their constitution was changed to say that only "brethren" could vote rather than the original gender-neutral "messengers."[14] Preceding women's right to vote in the United States by two years, the SBC altered their stance by giving women voting privileges in 1918. In 1964 Watts Street Baptist Church ordained the first Southern Baptist woman, Rev. Addie Davis, in Durham, North Carolina.[15] In the thirty years that followed, many Southern Baptist churches ordained women and invited women into the pulpit in preaching ministry.

The main gendered controversy began to brew in the late 1970s when well-organized and heartily-financed fundamentalist evangelicals launched a plan to take over the Southern Baptist Convention.[16] Their motives hinged on their belief in the inerrancy of scripture, and embedded in the inerrancy of scripture is the subordination of women. By the 1990s the takeover was complete, and the SBC's primary document of faith, the Baptist Faith and Message, was being revised to reflect the new group's misogynistic view of gender. These revisions began with the 1984 Resolution, which states, "we encourage the service of women in all aspects of church life and work other than pastoral functions and leadership roles entailing ordination."[17] In 1998 Article XVIII was added and dubbed "The Family Amendment." The key concern in this amendment was putting women in their "rightful" and godly place in relation to men:

> The husband and wife are of equal worth before God. Both bear God's image but in differing ways. The

[14] Rob James and Gary Leazer, *The Fundamentalist Takeover in the Southern Baptist Convention* (Timiosoara: Impact Media, 1999), 47.
[15] James and Leazer, 47.
[16] Audra Trull and Joe Trull, eds., *Putting Women in Their Place* (Macon: Smyth and Helwys, 2003), viii.
[17] *Annual of the Southern Baptist Convention* 1984.

> marriage relationship models the way God relates to his people. A husband is to love his wife as Christ loved the church. He has the God-given responsibility to provide for, to protect, and to lead the family. A wife is to *submit graciously* to the servant leadership of her husband even as the church willingly submits to the leadership of Christ. She, being 'in the image of God' as is her husband and thus equal to him, has the God-given responsibility to respect her husband and serve as his "helper" in managing their household and nurturing the next generation.[18]

As if this antiquated understanding of gender was not enough, the SBC finalized their revisions to the Baptist Faith and Message in 2000, stating, "While both men and women are gifted for service in the church, the office of pastor is limited to men as qualified by Scripture."[19]

While this is the official patriarchal stance of the Southern Baptist Convention, it is not reflective of where many other Baptists stand on the issue. For example, the Progressive National Baptist Convention, an historically black Baptist group, affirms the ordination of women, as do the American Baptist Church USA, which grew out of the Northern Baptist Convention. Similarly, the Baptist Peace Fellowship of North America was founded 1984 to mobilize Baptists to stand for peace rooted in justice and they have always affirmed the ordination women and the LGBTQ community. So, too, have the Alliance of Baptists, a progressive Baptist movement officially named in 1992. And the more moderate Cooperative Baptist Fellowship does not condone LGBTQ inclusion, but it formed in large part based on gender equality in all aspects of ministry in 1991. Moreover, the Association of Welcoming and Affirming Baptists began in 1993 and also affirms the ordination of women and the LGBTQ community.

---

[18] *The Baptist Faith and Message* (Nashville: LifeWay Christian Resources), 13. *Italics mine.*

[19] *The Baptist Faith and Message*, 13.

The controversy that erupted in Baptist life parallels the status of women in ordained ministry in many other denominations. Sexists proclaim that a woman preaching from a pulpit is distracting because her beautiful outward appearance would cause (straight) men to lust, or because the timbre of her voice is too high, or because she is too emotional to properly interpret scripture and proclaim the Word. If these reasons are not absurd and misogynistic enough, some even claim that women are too small to be seen behind massive pulpits. These "reasons" not only essentialize women's "feminine" attributes in markedly negative ways, but they are utterly archaic and bigoted in nature.

This glimpse into the history of preaching women in Baptist life—while far from exhaustive—reminds us of two important factors that impact the gendering of the pulpit. On the one hand, we are reminded that patriarchy is alive and well, continuing to exclude, marginalize, and oppress based on bigoted interpretations of scripture. On the other hand, the SBC controversy also reminds us that the pulpit has not always been gendered in sexist ways. Women were once ordained and affirmed and that right was taken away in relatively recent history. We can surmise, therefore, that it has not always been this way. And it does not always have to be this way. Each time a woman steps into the pulpit—before she utters a word—her gendered body subverts these sexist traditions that seek to render women mute. This gendered preaching event has happened throughout history; it happens today; and its happenings are theological.

Theology and the Gendered Pulpit

Where did your Christ come from? From God and a woman. Man had nothing to do with him.[20]

Over the past fifty years feminist, womanist, and mujerista theologians have shaped our understanding of God, the Spirit, Jesus, the church, and humanity. Such women have much to contribute to gendering the pulpit. Over-viewing the role of

---

[20] Sojourner Truth, "Ain't I A Woman," in *Feminism*, ed. Schneir (New York: Vintage Books, 1972), 94.

theology in preaching and worship is not the specific aim of this book, however. Rather, exploring how gender constructs the sermon and how the sermon constructs gender is our goal. In order to reach this goal theologically, I find it important to narrow our focus to the gendered body, and specifically the gendered body of Jesus. Consequently, I'd like to take a glimpse at feminist understandings of the incarnation.

In *White Women's Christ and Black Women's Jesus*, Jacquelyn Grant overviews the contribution of white feminists to the so-called problem of Jesus' maleness, while beginning to construct a womanist response to this incarnational conundrum. She states, "It is my claim that there is a direct relationship between our perception of Jesus and our perception of ourselves."[21] If gendered, sexualized, and racialized bodies step into the pulpit and those elements of identity contribute to the construction of the sermon, then the gendered, sexualized, and racialized identity of Jesus must also be important. If Jesus is perceived as male, straight, and white, then what does that teach women, persons of color, or the LGBTQ community about embodied divinity? Feminist theologians have answered this question in myriad ways.

Mary Daly argues that because the person of Jesus is male, the male is recognized and celebrated as the superior being.[22] In these ways, the maleness of Jesus is something to be rejected or exorcised because Jesus' understood gender identity contributes to patriarchy and does not hold salvific power for women. Rather than rejecting Jesus altogether, Rosemary Radford Ruether asks the seminal question, "Can a male Jesus save women?"[23]

Jesus' gendered identity is an issue of incarnational theology because, according to the Christian tradition, God had to become human. So, God became flesh, just like you and me. But God did so in the person of Jesus, a male who appeared to

---

[21] Jacquelyn Grant, *White Women's Christ and Black Women's Jesus* (Atlanta: Scholars Press, 1989), 63.
[22] Mary Daly, *The Church and the Second Sex.*
[23] Rosemary Ruether, *To Change the World: Christology and Cultural Criticism* (New York: Crossroads Publishing, 1981).

fall into one side of the constructed gender binary, the side that has power and privilege: male. So, Ruether's question begs us to consider how one whose gendered body is afforded power and privilege can relate to those without power and privilege. Grant notes that for white feminists, "the doctrine of Christology, from its initial formulated inception has been problematic for women…the fact that the church teaches that God's incarnation is uniquely represented in the historical male figure Jesus, provided for the predominance of the one-sided Christological interpretation throughout the history of theology."[24]

Feminists like Letty Russell respond to Ruether's question through a liberation perspective by highlighting Jesus' universal participation in the new humanity. The maleness of Jesus is known as the "scandal of particularity"[25] because his gender was constructed in a particular way. Russell notes that Jesus had to have been a man simply because of the patriarchal context in which he was born; his message would have been lost if Jesus was born into the body of someone gendered female. So, Russell challenges women to disconnect Christ's work from his maleness. Jesus' gender, according to this perspective, is not as important as his message of liberation and salvation. Therefore, the maleness of Jesus is merely incidental. The humanity of Jesus, however, is salvific.

In contrast, Rita Nakashima Brock does *not* think that a male Jesus can redeem woman, saying:

> If Christology is to be reclaimed in feminist visions, the image of an exclusive divine presence in a 'perfect' man called Jesus who came to be called the Christ is disallowed. The doctrine that only a perfect male form can incarnate God fully and be salvific makes our individual lives in female bodies a prison

---

[24] Grant, 83.

[25] Letty Russell, *Human Liberation in a Feminist Perspective* (Philadelphia: The Westminster Press, 1974), 137.

> against God and denies our actual, sensual, changing selves as the lover of divine activity.[26]

Brock proposes that Jesus, and his maleness, be decentralized in the Christian tradition so that the stories and experiences of women can come to the center. Still, Elizabeth Johnson revises traditional Christological understandings of Jesus by deeming him Jesus-Sophia, speaking about how wisdom is made flesh in the person of Jesus. This wisdom-in-flesh liberates what has previously been twisted into justification for patriarchal domination.[27]

Grant critiques these views by highlighting the way many white feminists have presumed a sisterhood of experience based on gendered oppression, while neglecting or ignoring the way women of color have also experienced oppression based on racialized identity. She explains that Jesus is understood in diverse ways in the womanist community, but primary is "the belief in Jesus as the divine co-sufferer, who empowers them in situations of oppression. For Christian Black women in the past, Jesus was their central frame of reference. They identified with Jesus because they believed that Jesus identified with them. As Jesus was persecuted and made to suffer undeservedly, so were they."[28] Before Alice Walker ever coined the term "womanism,"[29] an abolitionist and women's rights activist who escaped slavery articulated poignantly this Christological debate and the ways white feminists ignored the plight of black women. At the 1851 Ohio Women's Convention, Sojourner Truth raised her voice to proclaim one of the most nuanced and powerful "sermons" about incarnation ever uttered:

> Then that little man in black there, he says women can't have as much rights as men, 'cause Christ

[26] Rita Nakashima Brock, "The Feminist Redemption of Christ," in *Christian Feminism*, ed. Judith Weidman (New York: Harper and Row, 1984), 68.
[27] Johnson, 150-151.
[28] Grant, 212.
[29] Alice Walker, *In Search of our Mothers' Gardens: Womanist Prose* (New York: Harcourt, 1983).

> wasn't a woman! Where did your Christ come from? Where did your Christ come from? From God and a woman. Man had nothing to do with Him. If the first woman God ever made was strong enough to turn the world upside down all alone, these women together ought to be able to turn it back, and get it right side up again! And now they is asking to do it, the men better let them.[30]

Grant nuances this beautiful argument further, noting that today, the Christ who is found in the experiences of black women is a black woman. Jesus is incarnate, gendered, and racialized as a black woman.[31] Or, as many thoughtful theologians have proclaimed, Jesus was a male, yes, but the Christ could be a woman.

These gendered, sexualized, and racialized identities send a message before a preacher even opens her mouth; they are not identities that the preacher can take off when she steps into the pulpit. Similarly, the gendered, sexualized, and racialized identity of Jesus also preaches a message about what bodies are valued, affirmed, and even redeemed. In order to gender the pulpit in the direction of justice, the preacher has compensating to do. The presence of her gendered body in the pulpit is a first step in compensating or repairing the way women have been oppressed throughout the ages. The gendered body—without even speaking—takes a step toward redemption. But what is spoken is also a vital part of gendering the pulpit. In the next section, the words uttered by preachers and liturgists are the central focus.

Preaching, Worship, and the Gendered Pulpit

Gail Ramshaw speaks of the importance of inclusion in liturgical language, noting that liturgical language is one of many types of Christian speech. On the whole, liturgical language is not as idiosyncratic as the words of mystics, or as philosophical or argumentative as the speech of a systematic theologian, but it

---

[30] Truth, 94.
[31] Grant, 220.

is the primary form of speech that most Christians hear.[32] The words proclaimed, sung, prayed, and uttered during worship are the words that shape the faith of most Christians. These are the words that gender our pulpits. They have the power to subvert or encourage the patriarchal norm. Accordingly I would like to focus on the liturgical language proclaimed in liturgy and sermon.

When introducing the concept of inclusive language, Shannon Clarkson notes, "Only when one refers to the minister as 'he' and then sees a woman step to the pulpit does the speaker begin to reevaluate the generic use of 'he' for minister."[33] Inclusive language is defined in opposition to exclusive language. According to Sharon Warner, exclusive language is "defined as language which holds up one particular entity or reality as the norm for all other entities or realities; it functions to establish one particular as universal and generic. 'Inclusive language' is here defined as language which permits particulars."[34] When a preacher utilizes inclusive language, she recognizes the history of oppression embodied in gendered language for humanity and God. Accordingly, she uses her words to subvert and overturn such domination.

It is worth noting that I made a particular choice in referring to the preacher as "she" rather than a more neutralized s/he; some might even claim that my word choice is ironic in a section about inclusive language because it chooses to include "she" at the expense of "he." Is this choice exclusionary? Sharon Warner's work on the particularity of inclusive language offers a helpful response to such statements of exclusion.

Warner notes that inclusive language falls into two categories. The first is inclusive language that is neutral. The second is that which is particular. Most churches, denominational bodies, or seminaries that promote the use of

---

[32] Gail Ramshaw, *Liturgical Language* (Collegeville: Liturgical Press, 1996), 5.

[33] Shannon Clarkson, "Inclusive Language and the Church," *Prism: A Theological Forum for the UCC* 5:2 (Fall 1990): 46.

[34] Sharon Warner, "The Value of Particularity: Inclusive Language Revisted," *Lexington Theological Quarterly 29:4* (Winter 1994): 249.

inclusive language choose the first option. In these cases, preachers and liturgists use gender neutral language, such as "human," "humankind," "person," "people," etc. when referencing groups of men, women, children, etc. An exclusive example of describing this same group would be to call them all "men" or "mankind." Since Webster's Dictionary deemed it academically archaic to refer to a group of humans as "men" in 1971, suffice it to say that the church is a bit behind the curve. When a preacher or liturgist chooses to utilize neutral inclusive language, the words function at the level sameness, erasing any notions of particularity. On the other hand, a preacher or liturgist could use particular inclusive language by utilizing terms such as "men and women," "children and adults," etc. Particular inclusive language invokes variety, specifically a variety of particulars which do not attempt to neutralize the whole in a universalizing way.[35] Warner contends that neutrality is not enough. She nuances her argument further in a way that elucidates how to gender the pulpit by highlighting particularity; her comments are worth recounting at length:

> Particular inclusive language for reference to God needs further exploration here. *Please,* hear me clearly. The philosophy of inclusive language does critique the use of the particularity of Father language for God as exclusive. However, the critique of Father language for God is *not* that it is exclusive by virtue of its being particular, but that it is exclusive by virtue of its claim to being universal. Father language for God functions oppressively for many people by virtue of its claim to serve as the normative particular which all should have. Thus, the problem with Father language for God is *not* that it expresses a particular view of God. That is its power and that is what must be claimed. But, its particularity must be exposed. For too long its particularity has been *masked* as it has been promoted as a universal and generic view of God. When particularity is masked it is never problematized. We never see that there might be a problem with this particular (or any particular)

[35] Warner, 250.

> functioning as a name for God. As many have noted, our failure to problematize a particular leads to idolatry, to equation of that particular with God. To expose the particularity of Father language for God we need to place it alongside many other particular names and images, for only alongside many other particulars can it be seen as *only* one other particular and, therefore, as participative in the human problem of calling God by any name.[36]

Karen Stroup bolsters Warner's claim by emphasizing what most congregants actually hear or think of when neutralized inclusive language is employed in liturgy. Stroup suggests that when we carefully replace "He" and "His" with "God" and God's," most people still hear with their internal perceptive ear "He" and "His" because referencing God in this way has been normalized and universalized for centuries.[37] Marjorie Procter-Smith agrees, saying, "Gender-neutral referents tend to be heard as male unless they are stereotypically female. The use of *God* as if it were gender-neutral does not challenge the prevailing belief that God is male."[38] In these ways, neutral inclusive language continues to allow socialized patterns of domination to shape perceptions of God and humanity. If men and women were truly treated equally, and if an equal number of people perceived God to be female as male, then such neutral language could work. But women and men are not treated equally in society, and certainly not in the church, and most people still perceive God in male terms. Until this shifts, neutral language is not sufficient enough to gender the pulpit in the direction of justice.

I have shared such perspectives with many congregants in many congregations, proclaiming them from the pulpit in a way that was liberating for many. In some cases, however, someone inevitably brings up charges of a "double standard,"

---

[36] Warner, 251.

[37] Karen Leigh Stroup, "God Our Mother: A Call to Truly Inclusive Language," *Lexington Theological Quarterly* 27 (January 1992): 12-13.

[38] Marjorie Procter-Smith, *In Her Own Rite: Constructing Feminist Liturgical Tradition* Nashville: Abingdon, 1990), 91. As quoted in Warner.

claiming that such particular language risks reverse sexism, or that it excludes the voice of men. Since I often cannot keep my cool in such situations and simply want to cry, "Since when are men's voices excluded? How are men an oppressed or marginalized minority in the church or society?" I will turn again to the thoughtful nuance of Warner's argument for particularity.

First, she explains that claiming a particularity is not oppressive. So, calling God "Mother" is not oppressive to men. But to claim that a particularity is universal is to oppress. So, calling God "Mother" at the expense of "Father" in a world where "Mother" is the common understanding of God would be oppressive to men. But we do not reside in such a world. "Indeed, anyone religiously formed in this era experiences the Mother image as a particular, not as a universal. Reverse oppression, or any oppression, is not what is happening here."[39] Second, the historic male language for humanity and God has functioned oppressively in ways that keep women from flourishing, prevent women from ordination, and sustain all-male power structures (ie: the all-male priesthood, for example). Warner concludes, saying, "The probability in the use of feminine language for God for a similar oppression of men is dubious given the continual male dominated social and religious life in which we reside. In this present historic context, the preferential cultivation of what has been silenced, specifically feminine images of God, functions to balance not to oppressively exclude."[40]

I contend, like I did in the previous section on theology, that the preacher has some compensating to do. This conversation would look very differently if women and men were treated, ordained, and given opportunities to preach equally. If such were the case, there would be no need to compensate, no need to gender the pulpit. Until all pulpits—and all of society—are gendered in the direction of justice and equality, an inclusive language of particularity must be employed in liturgy and preaching.

---

[39] Warner, 257.
[40] Warner, 257.

Practical Application: Sermon and Liturgy

Incorporating inclusive language that honors particularity is a vital part of gendering the pulpit. But the theories undergirding inclusive language are not enough. Sometimes clergy need ways to practically approach gender and inclusivity in worship and preaching. Accordingly, in this section I offer two practical applications. The first are a series of liturgical elements created for addressing the issue of gender within the context of worship. The second is a sermon that addresses gender.

Liturgical Elements Addressing Gender

Litany of Repentance and Assurance of Pardon

> For the times when we fail to acknowledge the complexities of our gendered identity,
> *Forgive us, Mother God.*
> For the times when we essentialize others, categorizing their complex identities into divisive binaries,
> *Forgive us, Father God.*
> For the times when we elevate one gender, while lowering another,
> *Forgive us, Lover God.*
>
> We know that You are our Co-Sufferer, one who knows what it is like to be misunderstood.
> *Liberate us, we pray.*
> We know that Your grace is bigger than the categories we use to bind humanity.
> *Liberate us, we pray.*
> We are confident that You love us in the midst of our differences.
> *Liberate us, we pray.*

Pastoral Prayer

God of many names, who is not constrained by gender or the binaries humans construct, thank you for the diversity that You imbue in each of us, Your beloved children. We are grateful that

You love unabashedly and without discrimination, celebrating the wondrous diversity of humankind: women, men, trans, gay, straight, bi, lesbian, queer, and those not limited to the finitude of our language. In a world where many of us feel constrained by socially constructed categories, we implore you to set us free. In a world where some are valued more than others, we beg you to liberate, overturn, subvert the status quo. And we ask you to embolden us to liberate, overturn, and subvert. Empower us to be Your people, people called to set the captives free, basking in Your never-ending, life-changing, always-accepting love that unites us all. Mother, Father, Friend, Lover, and Guide, incarnate Yourself in us we pray. Amen.

Music

Rather than list the hymn tunes and words for a few inclusive-language hymns that acknowledge the complexity of gender, I would like to briefly draw our attention to the language of the *New Century Hymnal*.[41] This hymnal includes some of the older hymns that are deeply meaningful for people, along with new and global hymns, while seeking to be inclusive and diverse. Accordingly, the *New Century Hymnal* addressed a variety of categories related to language: archaic language, the gender of God, use of "Father" for God, balancing masculine and feminine images, use of "Mother" and other feminine images for God, masculine pronouns for God, gender of Jesus Christ, the use of "Lord" and "Sovereign," the use of "Lord" for God, the use of Son of God or Child of God, the use of kings, kingdoms, and masters, militaristic language, triumphalistic language, language about the trinity, language that includes women, children, and men, the use of the word "dark," language about people's abilities, language that recognizes varied human experience, and language of science and technology. As you can see, their efforts at inclusivity and diversity are certainly not limited to issues of gender. Rather, the *New Century Hymnal* seeks to celebrate how worshipping communities are filled with

---

[41] Kristen Forman, ed., *The New Century Hymnal Companion* (Cleveland: The Pilgrim Press, 1998). In particular see pages 15-58.

a diversity of genders, races, ethnicities, sexualities, backgrounds, languages, abilities, and beliefs.

In many cases, this simply entailed reworking exclusive wording to make it more inclusive and contemporary. In other cases, however, it involved going back to the original language and discovering inclusivity previously lost in translation. One beautiful gendered example is from the hymn "Of the Father's Love Begotten." The original fourth century Latin text was consulted, reading "*Corde natus ex parentis*," which means "born from the heart of the parent."[42] Paying thoughtful and careful attention to the power of the words in hymns can gender the pulpit in the direction of justice. Sometimes it involves reworking the original text to make it inclusive and sometimes it involves discovering that inclusion was present all along.

Sermon Addressing Gender

This sermon, "Unfit, Unwed, and Utterly Favored," was preached on the last Sunday of Advent at Wake Forest Baptist Church in December 2011. In addition to the traditional Advent decorations that filled Wait Chapel—Advent wreath and candles, trees, blue and purple fabrics—there were four giant paintings of pregnant women hung in the space. On each of the four Sundays of Advent, another painting was added. Impressionist in nature, larger-than-life in size, the four seemingly abstract women were an array of deep reds, purples, and browns. Their bellies bulged. Their backgrounds were blue and white. Each was painted by an artist in the congregation when she was pregnant over twenty years prior. She did not paint them for Advent, but when she invited me to see some of her paintings and I caught a glimpse of these four, I immediately thought of the season. The paintings were pregnant with purpose and potential, expectation and longing. I preached this sermon in dialogue with these paintings, walking between and among them, sometimes even gesturing like the figures in the paintings.

---

[42] Forman, 26.

Unfit, Unwed, and Utterly Favored
The Fourth Sunday of Advent, Year B, Luke 1:26-38

Advent manifests itself in a variety of ways: Deep blues and purples of the candles, the vestments, the fabrics, the night sky; A tiny glimmering star that provides light in the darkness; A corporate song: *O Come, O Come, Emmanuel*; The night skies of Van Gogh that swirl across our bulletin covers each week; The Advent wreath, growing brighter—candle by candle—each Sunday; Peace, hope, joy, and love flickering among us; The artwork that surrounds us, pregnant with purpose, pointing us toward what it means to birth the light of love in our world.
[Move to stand between two pregnancy paintings]

Art, design, color, music, poetry: all bear witness to the season of Advent. Standing among these monoliths, mortals whose bellies have grown, filled with burgeoning life and love and potential, "Greetings favored one," the angel Gabriel tells a shivering young girl who had not planned on expanding her family or birthing a baby, let alone a god. Among their stories—of birth announcements, gestation, fear, and unabashed joy—I turn to another Advent manifestation, a poem by Kathleen Norris, entitled *Advent*.

They are fruit
and transport:
ripening melons,
prairie schooners journeying
under full sail.

Susan worries that her water will break
on the subway. New York is full of grandmothers;
someone will take care of her.
Kate has been ordered to bed.
A Wyoming wind like wild horses
brushes snow against her window.
Charlotte feels like a ripe papaya.
"The body's such a humble thing," she says,
afloat in her kitchen
in Honolulu,
unable to see her feet.

Pregnant women stand like sentinels,

they protect me
while I sleep. They part the sea
and pass down the bloody length of it,
until we are strangers
ready to be born,
strangers who will suffer and die.

They are home
and exile, beginning and end,
end and means.
I am more ordinary. Still, I listen
as the holy wind breathes through them.
I make a little song
in praise of bringing forth.[43]

[Move to other paintings, singing "O come, O come, Emmanuel. And ransom captive Israel. That mourns in lonely exile here. Until the child of God appears."]

"Greetings favored one." Mary looks left. She looks right. The poor, unwed teenage mother becomes "favored one?" There are a lot of places we could go with this Advent text. A lot of commentators speak of the virgin birth, though I resonate most with the thoughts of Marcus Borg, who claims that birth stories are rarely historically factual, but are profoundly true in another and more important sense. So, we could talk about how the virgin birth is not so much history remembered as it is a metaphorical narrative that uses ancient religious imagery to express central truths about Jesus' significance. But that's a little controversial for the holidays, don't you think?

So, this Advent text could also lead us to talk about the innate essentialism embedded in many feminist readings of the text. Many women highlight the story of Mary as an example of the divine feminine nature of God, gestating in the womb and birthing the sacred into being. And this is a powerful, albeit squeamish way of talking about divine incarnation, of God

[43] Kathleen Norris, "Advent," quoted in *Imaging the Liturgical Year*, eds. Susan Blain, Sharon Iverson Gouwens, Catherine O'Callaghan, and Grant Spradling, vol. 3 (Cleveland: United Church Press, 1996), 94.

enfleshing Godself into earthly reality through the expanding womb of young Mary.

Along these lines, Marcia Mount Shoop expounds upon Jesus' birth in her book about embodiment and the body of Christ called *Let the Bones Dance*. She writes:

> *Has anybody ever thought about Mary having contractions?*
> *Yes, she had contractions.*
> *But there is just that one line, something like...*
> *"and then the time came that she would be delivered" or whatever.*
> *She had Jesus in a barn, for Christ's sake.*
> *She had to let out at least a few shrieks along the way.*
>
> *Has anybody ever acknowledged that Mary had a cervix,*
> *much less that it dilated and was all stretched and bloody?*
> *What was it like for her?*
> *What was it like for her?*
> *Breathing, sweating,*
> *gripping whatever was closest to her determined hand...*
> *What was it like to labor with God that way?*[44]

And these words have power, power of overcoming our Docetic desires that sterilize Jesus' birth, that wipe away the manure in the manger, and instead birth a squeaky clean Christ into a Renaissance painting where Mary's porcelain flesh shimmers under her blue embroidered Shakespearean gown as she holds a white baby Jesus whose golden hair matches the halo around his clean head. We don't really want to think about the holy's cervix, let alone talk about it in worship. But it's there, dilated and pushing, groaning the light of love into the world.

Meister Eckhart says, "For all eternity, God lies on a birthing bed, giving birth. The essence of God is Birthing." So,

---

[44] Marcia Mount Shoop, *Let the Bones Dance* (Louisville: Westminster John Knox, 2010), 72-73.

we could continue to talk about these things—also quite controversial. But they're just as problematic as that virgin birth discussion because, while it's sometimes difficult to speak of Mary's cervix, it's easy to essentialize what it means to be woman and to equate women's holiness with their capacity to give birth. As we feminists struggle to elevate Mary and empower the role of women in scripture, and especially in relation to Jesus, we sometimes forget that speaking of birth and gestation is not always empowering or even essential to womanhood. Advent's waiting and longing is a stark reminder to many women and men who long for parenthood, who desire a belly-full of divinity, who wait patiently for birth to no avail. Further, it's too easy to assume that this is the ability or desire of all women.

There are many women out there, myself included, who do not have the ability to birth children, who will never know the essence of God if the essence of God is birthing. This does not make their bodies any less worthy, any less holy. Moreover, there are many women out there who desire to be parents, but discriminatory legislation prevents them from adopting children. As Elizabeth and I are in the research phase of adoption, we are starkly aware that North Carolina only allows one gay parent to adopt a child and, unless discriminatory laws change, the other one of us will never ever legally be our future child's mother. The host of implications for this discrimination are theological, for sure, but also very scary.

There are countless women and men out there who would beg to hear those beloved words, "Greetings favored one," and to know that Someone has looked upon their humble state and that parenthood is within their grasp. And there are countless women out there who, like Mary, are "with child" unexpectedly, unannounced, unplanned, and they would love and long to hear that they are not alone in this.

Amidst these controversies...of virgin births and essentialism and feminism and womanhood and aloneness, the connecting thread is the growing and changing human body. The incarnation, the birth of Jesus in the flesh, is a central tenant of Christianity, after all. It is that which we wait upon eagerly during this season of Advent. It is what is announced by the angel Gabriel to young Mary. Incarnation is a perfect combination of earthly normality and divine mystery. It's dirty. Messy. Grounded. Pregnant. And very real. "Divine mystery and earthy groundedness swirl about, creating new life that is knit together with the pieces of what already is. Pregnant bodies carry theological weight."[45]

Pregnant bodies carry theological weight. The body of a poor young girl, unexpectedly with-child, carries theological weight. Debbie Blue speaks of the audacity of this Advent story, the wild story of an unwed teenage mother sneaking its way into many a traditional narratives when she says, "Patriarchal fundamentalist households admit the pregnant mother, birthing god into their households at Christmas. So do syncretistic Brazilian jungle cults and uptight Swedish Lutherans. It's so outrageous, and beautiful, and somehow unifying." Who would have thought that someone who would likely be deemed an "unfit mother" today would birth the light of love into our world? Who would have thought that the unwed teenage mother would change the course of history?

"Greetings favored one," the angel Gabriel told the perplexed girl. Light and love will enter the world through your belly. A gift is given; love has arrived; you shall dwell in darkness no more. From hence forth, when you encounter someone you think to be unfit, unwed, unworthy, unclean, unessential, welcome them accordingly, by saying, "Greetings favored one," and crying…

[Move to center, singing, "O come, O come, Emmanuel. And ransom captive Israel. That mourns in lonely exile here. Until the child of God appears."]

There are captives that must be released. There are those mourning who must be comforted. Those in exile must be returned. The child of God appears…in each of us. "Greetings favored one," is all we long to hear. Amen.

Conclusions

How does the act of preaching construct gender and how does gender construct the sermon? The pulpit is gendered

---

[45] Shoop, 66.

through personal narratives, scripture, history, theology, inclusive language in preaching and worship. The pulpit is gendered in the direction of justice when we recognize that our gendered, sexualized, and racialized bodies preach a message before we even open our mouths. When women stand up to patriarchy, uncover gendered words embedded in scripture, form community with other inclusive and affirming denominations, overturn the particularity of the incarnation, and utilize inclusive language that values the particular, we gender the pulpit in the direction of justice. It turns out that "little girls" have had something important to say—something important to preach—all along. We just haven't been listening.

Chapter 4

Sexuality and the Body: Preaching, Worship, and Sexuality

THE ISSUE OF SEXUALITY—AND HOMOSEXUALITY in particular—has been beyond taboo in preaching and worship for centuries. If we are going to gender the pulpit in the direction of justice, we must be willing to address the complexities of sexuality honestly and prophetically. I aim to focus on homosexuality in particular through the lens of my personal experience as a lesbian, scripture, history, theology, and theories in preaching in worship. After sharing a personal story and these theoretical elements, I'll offer two practical ways for approaching the topic of homosexuality in preaching and worship. I begin with the mailbox at my church office…

Hate Mail

As an ordained Baptist lesbian I am relatively accustomed to receiving hate mail. On any given month, between my email and the church's mailbox I typically receive about three or four pieces of it. Granted, there are some months that are quiet and I hear nothing. And during some months the inbox and mailbox overflow with vitriol. It's frustrating, for sure, but it's usually something I can handle. The same six bible verses that I will discuss later in the scripture section are often cited in these letters. They rarely have a return address on the envelope. Sometimes the writers of these letters call me mean names like Jezebel, false prophet, or dyke. One of them described the way my flesh would smell when I was burning in hell. One said that I deserved to be raped so that I would learn to love men. One told me that I should be at the other end of a shooting range. None of these compare to a letter I received in fall of 2012.

Between preparing for the church to march in the local Pride parade and the publication of an open letter I wrote to Dan Cathy, COO of Chic-fil-a, after his statements against gay marriage, my hate mail increased in both volume and fervor. One letter stands out from all the rest. It was postmarked in Texas, but there was no return address or signature. In my letter to Dan Cathy, I mentioned that my partner and I are in an adoption process in the same way that many in his family have been involved in adoption. The person in this letter latched onto that part of my life and after including all the usual rhetoric—sinner, lesbian, lusts of the flesh, destined for hell, repent, leading my flock astray—he took the words too far. For the first time, my hate mail caused me to weep and feel afraid. For the first time, I questioned my calling to be a prophet for justice and equality and wondered if it might just be easier to keep quiet.

The person in the letter began to describe all the disgusting, unacceptable reasons why my partner and I would want to adopt a child. The writer couldn't fathom that we want a family just like many other couples. Instead, the writer of this particular piece of hate mail focused on the undeserved stereotype heaped upon the LGBTQ community, equating homosexuality with pedophilia. I was disgusted. I was horrified. I was truly hurt and afraid. I cried out on social media, simply reminding friends and colleagues to choose love instead of hate.

I share this part of the story simply to highlight some of the things countless LGBTQ people face on a regular basis. On top of discriminatory legislation—inability to marry, adoption restrictions, inability to file joint taxes with one's partner, the possibility of being fired simply for being gay in over half the states in our country, lack of protection against hate crimes, etc—LGBTQ people are also maligned in ways that assault our spirits, tear at our emotions, and even attack our families. Never before had my partner, or our future child, been the topic of my hate mail. I can take the hate, but I will not tolerate it impacting my family.

Fortunately, the story does not end with hate, though I do still receive my fair share of hate mail. Rather, as a response to my crying out on social media, a friend and colleague from Baptist Women in Ministry organized a letter writing campaign. I had no idea she was doing this. About a week after reading the most venomous hate mail I'd ever received, our church administrative assistant walked into my office with a big grin on his face. "I have some letters for you," he told me. I rolled my eyes and braced myself for more hate. "Look," he said, pointing to the return address on one envelope, "it has a return address." He turned the envelope over, "and a pink heart sticker," he noted, pointing to the sticker that sealed the envelope. I raised my eyebrow. One at a time, he dropped envelopes on my desk, all complete with return addresses. One, two, three…I began to lose count. That day over ten arrived. They were all "love letters" written by clergy and laity affiliated with Baptist Women in Ministry. Over the next month, they kept coming. I stopped keeping count at thirty-five.

The majority of these writers were people I had never met. They included words of encouragement, scripture, and affirmation. One came from a seminary student who enclosed two necklaces crafted by women in Uganda; she admonished me and my partner to wear them as amulets, as a way of warding off evil and hate. One came from a mother who shared my story with her four-year-old daughter. She explained to her daughter that some people were being very mean to me and writing me nasty notes because I loved a lady and lived with the lady as my wife. Her young daughter contributed to her letter by drawing a picture of a purple and green heart with words printed boldly across the bottom in pencil, "God loves you." One love note was written on a postcard that read, "I'm the Preacher Your Mother Warned You About." I taped it to my office door.

To me, this story is representative of what it's like to gender the pulpit in the direction of justice, for my sexuality to step boldly with me into the pulpit and proclaim the Word with my sexualized body. Ordained. Lesbian. Preacher. No hate mail can take that away. But this story, like the experience of gendering the pulpit toward justice, is twofold, isn't it? On the one hand, there is the hate mail, the vitriol, being featured as the demon in another pastor's newsletter, the way that people who have never even met you think they can describe your character based solely on who you love. Sometimes those things can be overwhelmingly scary and hurtful. Sometimes they can even make you question your calling to acts of prophetic justice. On the other hand, there are those beautiful love letters. There is the knock on your door, less than one day after you shared the news of that horrible hate mail, and a straight ally is standing on your porch with freshly baked cookies. "When I get angry, I bake," she tells me. "It's ok. I'm really used to it by now," I tell her gratefully. "But you shouldn't have to be!" she shouts. "I know they're only cookies, but I hope that when you eat them you'll remember that you are loved and affirmed and when you preach you make us all better and more loving people."

So it is. No one said that gendering the pulpit in the direction of justice was easy. No one said that being a lesbian preacher was without pain and opposition. Amidst the pain and vitriol, the injustice and blatant discrimination, those cookies sure tasted sweet.

Scripture and the Sexualized Pulpit

When preachers spew exclusion from the pulpit, or Christians cite qualifications for the condemnation of the LGBTQ community, the reason most often given is scripture. How many times have we seen Fred Phelps and the members of Westboro Baptist Church marching with signs that read, "God Hates Fags," with Leviticus18: 22 or 20:13 plastered across them? There are many good books and solid scholars that address the "big six" texts most often used against the LGBTQ community.[46] In order to faithfully discuss how to gender the

---

[46] Some illustrative examples include John Boswell, *Christianity, Social Tolerance, and Homosexuality* (Chicago: Chicago University Press, 1980), Jeffrey Siker, *Homosexuality in the Church* (Louisville: Westminster John Knox, 1994), Daniel Helminiak, *What the Bible Really Says about Homosexuality* (San Francisco: Alamo Square Press, 1994), Nicholas Coulton, ed., *The Bible, the Church, and Homosexuality* (London: Darton, Longman and Todd, 2005). Gregg Drinkwater, Joshua Lesser, and David Shneer, *Torah Queeries* (New York: New York University Press, 2009), Deryn Guest, Robert Goss,

pulpit in the direction of justice by including the voices of this oppressed community, I find it important to offer a brief overview of these six passages: Genesis 1-2, Genesis 19:1-9, Leviticus 18:22 and 20:13, Romans 1:26-27, 1 Corinthians 6:9, and 1 Timothy 1:10. Before delving into the creation narrative in Genesis, it is worth noting that Jesus never condemned homosexuality. Additionally, in all of scripture, which is filled admonitions about poverty, divorce, and justice, homosexuality is only tangentially referenced six times. It's interesting and disheartening to see how much controversy these six little texts can stir up.

Genesis 1-2. Perhaps you've heard the quip: "God created Adam and Eve, not Adam and Steve." This pithy saying undergirds the homophobic understanding of the creation narrative. It's worth noting that there are two creation narratives embedded in Genesis 1-2. The first does, indeed, state that God created them "male and female," though no admonition is offered regarding the relationship between this male and female. We do not read of marriage, a wedding, or even a covenant made between the male and female. This first creation story has not only been used to condemn gays and lesbians, but it has also been used within the gay and lesbian community to sometimes condemn transgendered persons. One of the foremost scholars of the Hebrew Bible, Walter Harrelson, had something to say about such faulty interpretations.

I had the great privilege of serving as pastor to the esteemed bible scholar Walter Harrelson for nearly two years. The summer preceding his death, he volunteered to teach a bible study for the young adult Sunday School class at our church. The topic was "Progressive Interpretations of Scripture." In his class sat one of our transgender members who asked our beloved and world-renowned bible scholar, Dr. Harrelson, about the Genesis story. This text had been used to hurt and exclude him on countless occasions. Rather than emphasizing the implicit gender binaries of Genesis 1, Walter focused on the creation story found in Genesis 2. Here, God creates *adamah*, literally a

---

Mona West, and Thomas Bohache, eds., *The Queer Bible Commentary* (London: SCM Press, 2006).

"mud creature" or "dust being" made from the earth, and God breathes life into this genderless creature. Once God breathes into *adamah, adamah* becomes a living being, a human. Gender identity and sexual orientation are not what the creation story is about. Rather, Genesis is about God breathing life into humanity and calling it "very good," creating beauty out of chaos and mystery and inviting us to dwell in that beautiful chaos and mystery together. When Dr. Harrelson passed away I invited congregants to write ten words about what he meant to them. From our member who sat beside Walter in that Sunday School class during summer of 2012 I received this note: "Walter Harrelson made it ok to be a transgender Christian."

Genesis 19:1-9. The story of Sodom and Gomorrah: two angels disguised as men arrive in town, Lot offers them hospitality by inviting them into his house, the people of the town demand that Lot release the men/angels so that the people may "know" them, Lot offers his daughters instead, the people continue to demand the angels/men, the angels strike the people blind, the towns are destroyed, Lot and his family are saved (with the exception of his wife). There are three things worth mentioning in relation to this story: 1) the word "know," 2) the references to this story elsewhere in scripture, and 3) the role of rape. First, Peter Gomes points out that the word for "know" in this story is used 943 times in the Hebrew Bible; in only ten instances does the word refer to "knowing" in the carnal or sexual sense. Additionally, in the ten instances when it is used to refer to sexual relations, none of those relations involve homosexuality.[47] While many claim that homosexuality is the sin of Sodom and Gomorrah—the justification for why the cities were destroyed by God—the reasons listed throughout scripture never mention homosexuality. Ecclesiastes cites pride as the reason for Sodom and Gomorrah's fall. Ezekiel sites a failure to help the poor and needy as the rational for God's destruction. And Jesus claims in both Matthew and Luke that Sodom was destroyed because the town lacked hospitality. Finally, even if the people of the town did desire to have homosexual sex with

---

[47] Peter Gomes, *The Good Book* (San Francisco: HarperSanFrancisco, 1996), 151-152.

the men/angels, we are missing the point of their sin if we claim that homosexuality is the problem. *Rape* is the problem. The people of the town did not desire to have consensual, mutual sex with the men/angels. They were beating down the door in order that they might gang rape them. Rape, whether perpetrated on a person of the same sex or a different sex, is heinous, surely an abomination before God and humanity.

Leviticus 18:22 and 20:13. The holiness code. Leviticus 18:22 reads, "You shall not lie with a male as with a woman; it is an abomination." And Leviticus 20:13 states, "If a man lies with a male as with a woman, both of them have committed an abomination; they shall be put to death, their blood is upon them." It is easy to pluck these terse statements out of their historical and priestly contexts, writing them boldly on a poster, and proclaiming that homosexuality is an abomination. To do so, however, is to neglect the context in which these texts were written, and also to misunderstand the ancient meaning of an abomination. These verses fall within the category of a holiness code. The holiness code is all about setting apart the Jewish people as a separate nation. Further, the Israelites were a small rag-tag bunch that desired to grow, flourish, and thrive. Therefore, anything that would either prevent them from growing or make them look more like their Canaanite neighbors was not permitted. For example, round haircuts, tattoos, or wearing fabrics made from different materials must have been all the rage in Canaanite culture because they were all condemned under the holiness code in Leviticus. So, too, were things that would prevent the growth of the nation. Examples include eating shell-fish because these crustaceans were understood to be harmful for your health; if you eat shrimp, get sick, and die, you will certainly not be contributing to the growth and health of your nation. Shell-fish, therefore, are an abomination. Additionally, if a man touches his wife while she is menstruating, his action is an abomination. The rationale is simple. If a man touches his wife, he may become so overcome with lust that he has intercourse with her. Having intercourse with a menstruating woman cannot result in childbirth, so this interaction will not help the nation grow. It is an abomination. So, there is a distinction between what is ritually impure and what is intrinsically wrong. Homosexuality, like touching a menstruating wife or eating shell-fish, is an abomination because it is ritually impure; it does not contribute to the building of a nation. A ritual impurity—an abomination—must not be equated with something that is inherently wrong, such as theft, rape, or murder. Claiming today that homosexuality is innately wrong because of proclamations from Leviticus is to misunderstand the text altogether. If homosexuality is wrong, so too, is eating shell fish, touching a menstruating woman, getting a tattoo, or wearing your hair in the shape of a bowl. As much as I would like for everyone to become vegetarian and quit wearing "bowl cuts," I simply don't think such proclamations are faithful understandings of the text.

Romans 1:26-27. All three of the New Testament texts can be interpreted within a Pauline understanding of homosexuality, so much of the explanation about Romans is applicable to Corinthians and Timothy, as well. Romans 1:26-27 states:

> For this reason God gave them up to dishonorable passions. Their women exchanged natural relations for unnatural, and the men likewise gave up natural relations with women and were consumed with passion for one another, men committing shameless acts with men and receiving in their own persons the due penalty for their error.

When we read verses like this in Paul's writings it is important to understand Paul's understanding of homosexuality and sin. In Romans Paul is writing about the fallen nature of humanity and how humans are ignoring God and following their own selfish desires. He continues to explain this fallen state by describing the Romans as evil, covetous, malicious, full of envy, murder, strife, deceit, malignity, calling them gossips, slanderers, haters of God, insolent, haughty, boastful, inventors of evil, disobedient to parents, foolish, faithless, heartless, and ruthless. This is the context in which Paul mentions unnatural relations in Romans 1. All of these dishonorable attributes are reflective of a fallen state where humans worship desire and passion rather than worshipping God. These unnatural relations do not describe homosexuals at all times in all places; rather, they describe that acts of heterosexual people who performed homosexual acts out of willfulness and fallenness. Paul's understanding of homosexuality was markedly different than homosexuality today. In today's culture, we witness same-sex couples in committed and covenantal relationships; Paul did not experience this. The "homosexuality" Paul referenced referred to prostitution and pederasty. Gomes highlights this point poignantly, saying, "All Paul knew of homosexuality was the debauched pagan expression of it. He cannot be condemned for that ignorance, but neither should his ignorance be an excuse for our own. To base the church's principled objections to homosexuality and homosexuals on the basis of Paul's imperfect knowledge is itself unprincipled..."[48]

1 Corinthians 6:9. These same arguments from Romans apply to the list of vices in Corinthians. Here, homosexuals are a part of a long list of individuals who will not inherit the kingdom of God, though much of this list focuses on immorality among heterosexuals, such as a man living with his father's wife. And you do not see anyone condemning heterosexuality based on the debauched version of it listed here. Again, Paul is referencing what he understood homosexuality to be, which stands in stark contrast to what homosexuality is today. Thus, those who prostitute young boys, and are willful, lustful, exploitive, avaricious, self-deceiving, self-absorbed, and idolatrous are not fit for heaven, according to Paul.

1 Timothy 1:10. 1 Timothy includes "sodomites" in the list of lawless and disobedient people. "Sodomite," however, refers specifically to a male prostitute. It is not a Pauline synonym for "homosexual." To cite 1 Timothy as a reason for condemning homosexuality is to misunderstand the use of the words in the text altogether. In this instance, Paul may be condemning male prostitution, but that is another topic for another time.

There is no doubt that many preachers who seek to gender the pulpit in the direction of justice and already affirm the LGBTQ community are tired are hearing these same debates over six hackneyed sets of scripture. No matter how tired we

---

[48] Gomes, 158.

become of queering these texts and explaining their historical contexts, people will continue to use these six pithy statements to malign, exclude, and marginalize the LGBTQ community. I wish there was no need to discuss the tired nuances of these texts in a book about gendering the pulpit toward justice. But there is. Until these texts are no longer used to bolster discriminatory legislation and exclude LGBTQ people from ordained ministry, we cannot stop talking about them. So, it is to the inclusion and exclusion of LGBTQ people in the history of the church that I now turn.

History and the Sexualized Pulpit

Rather than focusing on the history of the welcoming and affirming movement throughout all of denominational life, I find it important to once again focus on the particular. I have discovered that many people are quite surprised to learn that I am an ordained Baptist lesbian because most Baptists do not have a reputation for being LGBTQ-friendly. The group most widely known for protesting gay funerals is Westboro *Baptist* Church, after all. It is worth noting, however, that Westboro Baptist Church is not affiliated with a particular denominational body. Because of key principles in Baptist polity, namely the autonomy of the local church, Baptists are incredibly varied on an array of hot button issues. There is no denominational hierarchy that dictates right belief in the Baptist tradition. While there are sects and denominations under the Baptist umbrella that are adamantly against LGBTQ people, such as the Southern Baptist Convention, there are still many others that are affirming. The Baptist umbrella is very wide, after all.

Beginning on the far right, the Southern Baptist Convention (SBC) has passed several resolutions that reject the "homosexual lifestyle," and it also opposes same-sex marriage.[49] Similarly, American Baptist Churches USA (ABCUSA) holds that the practice of homosexuality is incompatible with Christian teaching, but the local congregations that make up ABCUSA vary widely on the issue and some churches choose to separate

[49] See, for example, the Southern Baptist Convention, "Resolution on Homosexuality," in June 1988.

from their regional body in order to welcome and affirm LGBTQ people. Both the National Baptist Convention and Progressive National Baptist Convention—two predominantly African American Baptist denominations—do not have official views or policies on the issue of homosexuality. The National Baptist Convention, however, notes that most of the churches in its membership would not ordain an "active" homosexual. Similarly, the Baptist Union of Great Britain paradoxically says same-sex couples should not be discriminated against, but that Christians who believe that these relationships are wrong should not be forced to compromise their beliefs.[50] For this reason, some believe that their position is a more moderate or neutral one.

Many have claimed that the Cooperative Baptist Fellowships (CBF) holds a more moderate view on homosexuality, as well, but I would propose that their official policy against hiring LGBTQ persons is just as exclusive as the others previously listed.[51] What is more, when the SBC attacked the CBF for their seemingly liberal stance by claiming that the CBF affirmed homosexuality, the former Coordinator Cecil Sherman responded by expressing his own views, highlighting that they were representative of most CBF participants. Sherman states that the bible teaches that homosexuality is a sin, that the gay interpreter of the bible twists the traditional meaning of the text, that gays can change, that local congregations should decide on the issue, and that the spirit of Jesus is needed in order to deal with gay or lesbian people.[52] This is hardly a neutral or moderate position. In fact, I would surmise that the way many moderate Baptists felt about the SBC's treatment of women in the 1980s and 90s is the way many progressive Baptists feel about the way the CBF is now treating the LGBTQ community. In recent years, the CBF has taken steps to discuss these issues

---

[50] See issues raised by the Equality Act at www.baptist.org.uk

[51] Don Hinkle, "CBF homosexuality stance ignites controversy over group's direction," *Baptist Press*,
October 27, 2000, http://baptist2baptist.net/printfriendly.asp?ID=187 [accessed January 18, 2013].

[52] Cecil Sherman, "About Homosexuality," *Baptist Today* (April 1, 1994), 23.

with more of an open mind, but their anti-gay hiring policy still stands.

With this sordid and exclusionary history in mind, one might wonder why and how I remain Baptist and lesbian. There are actually several open and affirming Baptist organizations that cling to the call for justice and equality for all. First and most notably is the Alliance of Baptists. In 1992 the Alliance of Baptists appointed a task force on human sexuality. After three years of discussion, the Alliance encouraged all of their member churches to "welcome all persons without regard to sexual orientation or marital status into the life of the congregation" and to "recognize and develop gifts for ministry in all persons without regard to sexual orientation."[53] In 2001, the Alliance grieved over the CBF's decision to implement an anti-gay hiring policy. And in 2004 the Alliance adopted a resolution in support of marriage equality. In so doing, the Alliance of Baptists became the first member of the National Council of Churches to go on record in support of same-sex marriage. The United Church of Christ joined them in their stance one year later.[54] In these ways, Baptists were on the cutting edge in LGBTQ affirmation, gendering the pulpit in the direction of justice long before many other progressive denominations.

The Alliance of Baptists is not alone in their inclusion of LGBTQ persons. Two years before the Alliance made its first resolution to accept and affirm LGBTQ persons into ministry, the Association of Welcoming and Affirming Baptists (AWAB) was established during the 1993 American Baptist Churches USA's Biennial meeting in San Jose, CA. Twenty local churches, three groups, and many individuals were charter members. AWAB grew out of a group called American Baptists Concerned for Sexual Minorities, which was founded in 1972 and merged with AWAB in 2003.[55] AWAB is the only Baptist

[53] Aaron Weaver, "Progressive Baptist Dissenters: A History of the Alliance of Baptists," http://www.allianceofbaptists.org/learn/about/history [accessed January 15, 2013].
[54] Weaver, "Progressive Baptist Dissenters: A History of the Alliance of Baptists."
[55] See http://www.awab.org/history.html [accessed January 18, 2013].

organization devoted solely to building the welcoming and affirming movement. They claim as part of their mission: "We work as individuals, congregations, regional groupings and as a national body to advance the Radical Welcome and Love of God in Jesus Christ through being the Ministry of Reconciliation and building up the Beloved Community where all will be one."[56] As of 2012, AWAB had seventy-six member congregations.

Joining the Alliance and AWAB is yet another Baptist organization devoted to LGBTQ affirmation: the Baptist Peace Fellowship of North America (BPFNA). The same year that the Alliance "came out" as an open and affirming organization, so too, did BPFNA. In 1995 they issued a Statement on Justice and Sexual Orientation that was unanimously approved by the BPFNA board of directors during their May meeting in New York City. In taking the stance to welcome anyone into the peacemaking movement, regardless of sexual orientation, BPFNA also made three pledges of LGBTQ activism:

- To work with our brothers and sisters to secure full civil and human rights within the larger culture and full participation within the body of Christ for those who have been excluded because of their sexual orientation;
- To encourage our larger Baptist family of faith, particularly within local congregations, to engage in open and vigorous dialogue - which includes the testimonies of gay/lesbian believers along with the study of Scripture - as we seek to discern the mind of Christ; and
- To oppose any action, statement or policy leading to discrimination or violence against people based on sexual orientation.[57]

Joining these three welcoming and affirming Baptist groups in North America is an organization from the United

---

[56] See http://www.awab.org [accessed January 18, 2013].
[57] See http://www.bpfna.org/sxorient [accessed January 18, 2013].

Kingdom: The Network of Baptists Affirming Lesbian and Gay Christians. Small and relatively unknown, this network seeks to be "supportive to lesbians and gay men and those with concerns about their sexuality within the church," and to "seek guidance of the Holy Spirit on these matters"[58] while encouraging the sharing of personal stories in order to foster understanding and inclusion.

While there are certainly some Baptists and other Christians who spew hateful rhetoric against the LGBTQ community, there are also many who have taken bold and prophetic stances on the issue. The Alliance of Baptists, Association of Welcoming and Affirming Baptists, Baptist Peace Fellowship of North American, and the Network of Baptists Affirming Lesbian and Gay Christians gender the pulpit in the direction of justice with their prophetic actions. In many cases, they have paved the way for other denominations to work toward affirmation, reconciliation, and welcome. There is no doubt that I have found solace and home with these Baptist groups, joining the other LGBTQ clergy who have not only been affirmed, but empowered to do the ministry of justice and equality. Westboro Baptist Church and the Southern Baptist Convention do not speak for all Baptists. Rather, there are other progressive and affirming Baptists who have boldly raised their voices on behalf of oppressed and marginalized communities, creating pathways for LGBTQ persons to step into the pulpit and proclaim a theology of radical inclusivity.

Theology and the Sexualized Pulpit

The role of sexuality in gendering the pulpit is theological, to be sure. And the impact of queer theology is important. Beginning with Derrick Bailey[59] and John Boswell,[60] some theologians began addressing homosexuality in an

---

[58] See http://www.affirmingbaptists.org.uk/ [accessed January 18, 2013].

[59] Derrick Bailey, *Homosexuality and the Western Christian Tradition* (London: Longmans, Green, 1955).

[60] John Boswell, *Christianity, Social Tolerance, and Homosexuality* (Chicago: Chicago University Press, 1980).

affirming way as early as the 1950s. Taking a cue from liberation theology, other LGBTQ-affirmative theologians developed queer liberation theology. A few examples of LGBTQ liberation theologians include George Edwards,[61] Richard Cleaver,[62] and Michael Clark.[63] Lesbian theologians added their voices to the predominantly male conversation with the relational theologies of Mary Hunt[64] and Elizabeth Stuart.[65] Finally, LGBTQ theology evolved into queer theology, which seeks to dismantle the constructed binaries of gender and sexuality. Foundational to this movement is the provocative work of Marcella Althaus-Reid[66] and Gerard Loughlin.[67] All of these strands of development are important. Since this work deals with the sexualized body, more focused attention on incarnational theology within queer theory is central in gendering the pulpit in the direction of justice. Of primary importance in this incarnational discussion is the work of Patrick Cheng.

Cheng is a theology professor at the Episcopal Divinity School in Cambridge, MA, and an ordained minister in the Metropolitan Community Church. His thoughtful work in queer theology was first articulated in *Radical Love: An Introduction to Queer Theology,*[68] and his most recent book, *From Sin to Amazing Grace: Discovering the Queer Christ*,[69] will guide our understanding of how the incarnation can empower the embodied realities of LGBTQ persons in preaching and ministry.

---

[61] George Edwards, *Gay/Lesbian Liberation* (New York: Pilgrim Press, 1984).

[62] Richard Cleaver, *Know My Name: A Gay Liberation Theology* (Louisville: Westminster John Knox, 1995)

[63] Michael Clark, *A Place to Start* (Dallas: Monument Press, 1989).

[64] Mary Hunt, *Fierce Tenderness* (New York: Crossroad, 1991).

[65] Elizabeth Stuart, *Just Good Friends* (London: Mowbray, 1995).

[66] Marcella Althaus-Reid, *Indecent Theology* (London: SCM Press, 1997).

[67] Gerard Loughlin, ed. *Queer Theology* (Malden: Blackwell, 2007).

[68] Patrick Cheng, *Radical Love* (New York: Seabury Books, 2011).

[69] Patrick Cheng, *From Sin to Amazing Grace* (New York: Seabury Books, 2012).

As our discussion about the particularity of the incarnation reminded us in the previous chapter about gender, our perception of Jesus impacts the way we see and understand ourselves. How is the LGBTQ community to understand who Jesus is? Can Jesus be queer? If so, how might this impact the queer community? Cheng answers these questions by outlining how queer theology offers us seven different images of Jesus that can empower the LGBTQ community and gender the pulpit in the direction of justice, equality, and affirmation.

The first image is of Jesus as the Erotic Christ.[70] The Erotic Christ is the embodiment of God's deepest and most passionate desire for us. This is similar to Carter Heyward's "radically mutual character"[71] of Jesus Christ's life, death, and resurrection. This image of Jesus teaches us the power of mutuality, affirming sexuality as a vital part of faith. A second image is the Out Christ, which acknowledges that God "comes out of the closet" in the person of Jesus Christ and this "coming out" illustrates God's solidarity with the oppressed and marginalized. The Out Christ empowers the LGBTQ community to live fully, openly, and authentically into who they are without apology. The Liberator Christ is a third image. This liberating image understands Jesus as one who sets free those who are enslaved by heterosexism and homophobia. It liberates Christians from limiting gender identity or sexuality to constructed and limiting binaries. The Transgressive Christ composes the fourth image. This image acknowledges that Jesus was crucified because he refused to conform to the constraining standards of the religious and political authorities of his time. Consequently, the Transgressive Christ empowers us to live subversively outside of the bounds of society's rules for conformity and to transgress social and religious norms that are oppressive. The fifth image is the Self-Loving Christ. This image seems to contrast with the self-sacrificing Christ that is

---

[70] Note that the seven images of Jesus come from the seven chapters comprising part two of Cheng's *From Sing to Amazing Grace* unless otherwise noted.

[71] Carter Heyward, *Touching Our Strength: The Erotic as Power and the Love of God* (New York: HarperSanFrancisco, 1989).

often highlighted in theology. But it is worth noting that the Self-Loving Christ is one who loved himself enough to continue in ministry even in the most difficult circumstances. When Jesus calls us to love our neighbor as our self, for example, we must first love ourselves in order to love our neighbor. This model reminds us of the importance of self-worth and of loving ourselves even when others do not. In is no secret that pride and self-love is very needed by many in the LGBTQ community who are discriminated against and demoralized on a regular basis. A sixth model is the Interconnected Christ, which illustrates that Jesus is the one in whom all things interconnect—cosmos, ecosystems, spiritual traditions, etc. This version of Jesus encourages interdependence rather than isolation. And the final image is of the Hybrid Christ. Hybridity is a concept in postcolonial theory that describes the combining of two things that lead to a third thing, a hybrid. The Hybrid Christ, therefore, arises out of the understanding that Jesus is both divine and human in nature. This Jesus invites us into interstitial places of "in-between-ness." For example, one can be both queer and a person of color without forsaking or neglecting either aspect of the self.

Cheng's seven images of Jesus give the LGBTQ community an opportunity to see themselves in the person of Jesus. These images allow us to queer the pulpit and to embrace our sexualities as divine gifts that illuminate and inspire the proclamation of the Word rather than hampering it. Seeing ourselves in the person of Jesus is an important step in the LGBTQ community gendering the pulpit in the direction of justice, inclusion, and welcome. When the queer Christ enters into our preaching and worship, it is forever changed.

Preaching, Worship, and the Sexualized Pulpit

The sentiments of Siobahn Garrigan are ideal for beginning a section on preaching, worship, and the sexualized pulpit: "It is one thing for worship to be open to LGBT people, but it is quite another for it to be queer."[72] In the same way that I

[72] Siobhan Garrigan, "Queer Worship," *Theology and Sexuality* 15: 2 (May 2009): 223.

addressed the importance of queering theological understandings of the incarnation in the previous section, this section will briefly address the importance of queering worship and preaching.[73] It is worth noting that everything already discussed regarding the role of gender in preaching and worship in the previous chapter—namely inclusive language that addresses the particular—is also imperative to queering worship.

Several scholars have done interesting work creating queer rituals that address the particular needs of the LGBTQ community: same-sex unions, "coming out" ceremonies, or renaming ceremonies for individuals who have transitioned after gender reassignment.[74] However, as Garrigan contends, concentrating only on the extraordinary, occasional, or special events in a queer person's life ignores the way queer people also worship in everyday ordinary life in queer and subverted ways. There are queer rituals, to be sure, but that is not my focus here. Instead, I would like to emphasize ways in which regular Sunday morning worship can be queered.

Garrigan refers to this as "dismantling the heteronormative regime." Remembering that heteronormativity is rampant in society in general and that LGBTQ people live with the onslaught of homophobia on a daily basis is vital. As Janet Jakob-sen and Ann Pellegrini have stated: "From tax relief and inheritance rights to preferential treatment in immigration cases, state-sanctioned heterosexuality confers a host of material benefits and rewards. And all this in addition to the heterosexual couple's symbolic role as the nation's anchor, with the heterosexual family representing the body politic on a smaller

---

[73] For additional examples of queering worship see chapter two of Sharon Fennema's "Falling All Around Me: Worship Performing Theodicy in the Midst of the San Francisco AIDS Crisis," Ph.D. Dissertation, Graduate Theological Union, 2011.

[74] See Cherry Kittredge and Sherwood Zalmon, *Equal Rites: Lesbian and Gay Worship, Ceremonies, and Celebrations* (Louisville, KY: Westminster/John Knox Press, 1995); Paul V. Marshall, *Same-Sex Unions: Stories and Rites* (New York: Church Publishing, 2004); Elizabeth Stuart (ed.). *Daring to Speak Love's Name: A Gay and Lesbian Prayer Book* (London: Hamish Hamilton, 1992).

scale."[75] The prevalence of the heteronormative regime in daily civic life in America surely means that it seeps into our worshipping life, as well.

Some practical examples for queering worship include having the entire congregation involved in the process. One LGBTQ member or clergyperson cannot queer worship alone. If liturgy is truly "the work of the people," then the people must be committed to queering worship in meaningful, subversive, and empowering ways. Simple things, such as using sermon illustrations that involve LGBTQ people and issues can go a long way; not every example of a couple in a sermon has to be male and female, for example. Specifically saying the words lesbian, gay, bisexual, transgender, and queer from the pulpit or in hymnody can be empowering and liberating, a true embodiment of the "proclamation of the Word." In these ways, there are many words that need to be proclaimed and reclaimed. Avoiding heterosexist language or binaries in hymnody is also a possibility of gendering the pulpit in a queer way. In Advent, for example, perhaps the crooked pathways do not need to become straight. Perhaps the crooked pathways can become direct or plumb instead. Including a myriad of LGBTQ people in worship leadership is also important. Finally, do not mute the particular experiences of LGBTQ persons in order to fit normative liturgies. If the standard formulas for a baby dedication speak of a mother and father, for example, change them to honor the particular realities of queer people.

These liturgical possibilities for queering the pulpit are also evident in preaching. Primary in theorizing about queering preaching is Olive Hinnant.[76] Hinnant explores the concept of preaching through the metaphor of "coming out." "Coming out" as LGBTQ is akin to the preaching event in that both are spoken; the speech event, the proclamation of a/the word is central. Unlike many other marginalized groups, LGBTQ persons are not

---

[75] Janet Jakobsen and Ann Pellegrini, *Love the Sin: Sexual Regulation and the Limits of Religious Tolerance* (New York: New York University Press, 2003), 122.

[76] Olive Hinnant, *God Comes Out: A Queer Homiletic* (Cleveland: Pilgrim Press, 2007).

visibly identifiable. Our identity only becomes public through speech or action, such as referring to one's partner or showing affection to a person of the same-sex. Until one "comes out," names, or speaks one's identity, that individual is most often presumed to be hetero and, thus, a member of the dominant and accepted culture. Proclaiming otherwise changes everything. Consequently, "coming out" is a powerful metaphor for preaching because both are speaking events in which the speaker reveals something about God and something about the self, and in so doing, transforms the self by the speech-act. The preacher "comes out" when she integrates the fullness of her identity into her preaching.

In order to gender the pulpit in the direction of justice, worship and preaching cannot simply include LGBTQ persons. Gendering the pulpit fully involves queering preaching and worship. Recognizing the prevalence of heteronormativity in our regular worshipping life and then subverting, overturning, and dismantling it is the first step. Reconstructing it within the confines of a worshipping community that is committed to the radical inclusivity of queering worship is the second.

Practical Applications

In order to illustrate possibilities for queering worship and preaching in ways that gender the pulpit in the direction of justice, I offer two practical applications. The first is an assortment of liturgical elements that address some of the complexities of the LGBTQ community. The second is a sermon specifically about LGBTQ issues, though I would remind us that addressing LGBTQ issues is not limited to the one Sunday closest to Pride. Rather, since LGBTQ inclusion is a justice issue, it should permeate all of our preaching and worship on a regular basis.

Liturgical Elements

Prayer of Affirmation

Life Giver, Love Maker, Holy One in whom all things find worth and meaning, we are grateful that in you we are fearfully and wonderfully made. We are thankful that you do not make mistakes, but instead crafted our very being—every part of us—

with intentionality and care. We are your beloved works of art and nothing less. At times when we are treated as less than worthy, we ask for strength and empowerment. At times when we internalize that treatment and feel like less than a beautiful child of God, we ask for your compassionate reassurance. And at times when we fail to treat others as individuals made in your loving image, we ask forgiveness. Embolden us to walk justly. Empower us to stand tall, proud of what you have created—gay, straight, lesbian, bisexual, transgender, queer, or questioning—beloved and beautiful bodies in whom you delight. And strengthen us so that we might treat all humanity with the dignity, respect, and divine worth you imprint upon us. We pray these things in the name of peace, acceptance, welcome, and above all, love. Amen.

Music
Words by Pete Seeger, Stan Dotson, and Kim Christman
Tune: All People that On Earth Do Dwell (OLD HUNDRETH)

All people that one earth do dwell,
Sing out for peace 'tween heav'n and hell
'Tween East and West and low and high,
Sing! Peace on earth and sea and sky.

Between the white, black, red, and brown,
Between the wilderness and town,
Sing peace between the near and far,
'Tween Allah and six-pointed star.

Between the lesbian, gay, and straight
No longer we'll be bound by hate.
'Tween valley low and mountain tall
Lies one world open for us all.

All people that one earth do dwell,
Sing out for peace 'tween heav'n and hell
'Tween East and West and low and high,
Sing! Peace on earth and sea and sky.

Sermon

This sermon was preached in June 2009 at Shell Ridge Community Church in Walnut Creek, CA as thousands of people marched in the Pride parade in San Francisco. It was the same year the church voted to officially become an "open and affirming" congregation. All the statistics in the sermon are reflective of United States legislation as of summer 2009.

"Pride and Oppression"
2 Samuel 1:17-27
Mark 5:21-34

This morning I would like to share two stories with you: stories from scripture and stories from my own life. In fact, the two stories we've read from scripture had such a profound impact on my faith and theology that they shifted it altogether. Incidentally, both stories are our lectionary texts for today. The first story comes from the Gospel of Mark. It's the story of a woman. It's a story that I first read as a young woman who was recently handed a close-minded dose of Christianity, the kind of Christianity that says women are less than, unordainable, subservient. And since I had never experienced Christianity growing up, I set aside my feminist self and naively accepted this form of Christianity for a brief time. That is, until I read our text from Mark 5. Well, I suppose it wasn't quite this simple, but it was, indeed, my translation, exegesis, and experience with the New Testament texts that deal with the relationship between Jesus and women that changed my life and affirmed my call. Onto the story within my story: the story of a woman.

We don't know this particular woman's name. During her time, her name wasn't really that important. She was just a woman, and a sickly woman at that. Her place in society meant nothing. She was a nobody. At one time in her life she probably dreamed of her future: getting married, having children, growing old. She probably never imagined what life would be like if she didn't find a husband. Her options were slim. Either her father could take care of her into adulthood, which was highly unlikely. Or she could roam the streets. After all, women without husbands in that day and age were useless and only created a void in society.

This nameless woman's dream was probably so different than what her life had become. You see, this woman was sick. Very sick. She had been ill for twelve years. For twelve years she had been bleeding. And during that day and age, blood was not an option. It was unclean, impure. In fact, according to Leviticus 15 this woman was not allowed in the temple because she was ceremonially unclean due to her sickness. Priests couldn't go near her. No one could touch her, because if they did, they too would become unclean and be ostracized from the temple and community.

So, she sought help. For twelve long years she looked for physicians to heal her. For 4,380 days in a row she bled; she hurt. For twelve years she went without a family, a worship service, a touch. For 4,380 days this lonely woman did not receive a hug, a hand-shake, a high-five, a pat on the back, a touch. For twelve long years she searched, without the affirmation of a touch—never being touched by anyone. Ever. She couldn't go to friends for help. In fact, she probably didn't have many friends. You see, the community saw her as bad news. They felt that sin and disease went hand-in-hand. She must be sick because she's done something horribly sinful in her past. Her bleeding for twelve years must be the result of her inappropriate lifestyle. She couldn't go to priests for help, for they would become unclean. Furthermore, these priests didn't help women. According to the Rabbinic Tosefta, rabbis began each temple meeting by praying, "Blessed art Thou, O Lord, for Thou hast not made me a woman!" No help there!

She tried to go to doctors. According to Mark's account, she spent all she had on doctors and, instead of getting better, she felt worse. It's no wonder when we look at the Talmud's record of remedies for bleeding: garden crocuses dissolved in wine, sawdust from a lotus tree, ashes from an ostrich egg. If you ate those things, you'd probably feel worse too! No one could heal her: not friends, not rabbis, not doctors. It didn't even seem that she could ask God for help because, by law, she couldn't even go *in* the temple. So, Jesus solved that problem. He came *out* of the temple and into the streets where she could approach him one-on-one.

This nameless, bleeding outcast had heard of this Jesus character. What she heard must have been good because she traveled over thirty miles to see him—thirty miles without a bed to sleep in, a friend to chat with, a hand-shake from an acquaintance. Penniless, tired, sick, drained, and probably very sad she walked to find this one called Jesus. Something had to have kept her tired feet going.

After thirty miles, she arrived in Capernaum. Jesus was in a crowd of people and had just been stopped by Jarius, an elected ruler of the local synagogue, a man in power. Jesus was on his way to help Jarius's daughter. As he walked along the dusty road, mobs of people crowded all around him, all trying to catch a glimpse of what might happen next. In enters our nameless woman. The trip to Jarius's house would be interrupted, the plans would be disheveled, and a life would be touched forever. This silent woman, her face covered with the dirt from thirty miles and the tears of a dozen years, reached out an unclean hand. This woman steps out into the public arena, the arena that was considered the space of male power and male negotiations; and she takes action in this public place. She touches the fringe of the cloak of a Jewish rabbi surrounded by eager listeners. She has broken through the socio-cultural and religious barriers that would otherwise render her powerless. Will Jesus respond accordingly?

No. She touched and she would be touched—for the first time in twelve long years. We find that *immediately* she is freed from her suffering. Her bleeding stops. We discover that when she touches Jesus' robe that power left him. This word for power, strength, or miracle is the Greek word *dunamas*. From this word, we derive our English word for dynamite. Jesus did not just heal this woman. He empowered this woman. And then Jesus speaks. "Who touched me?!" he asks. Perhaps this was a kenotic moment for Jesus or perhaps he had a hunch and wanted to give this nameless woman a chance to break the silence. The disciples remind Jesus that the crowd is pressing in all around him and there is no way to know who touched him. I would speculate that at this time, Jesus looked into the teary eyes of our nameless woman and repeats his question: "who touched me?" And then our nameless woman breaks the silence. She is empowered and her voice will go unheard no longer. She speaks. She shares her story. And Jesus speaks again. Keep in mind that priests don't speak to women in public. I would imagine that this priest leaned over, held her tired hand, and spoke sweetly, "Daughter, your faith has healed you. Go in peace." Jesus noticed that this woman was worth stopping for. Worth listening to. Worth talking to. Worth healing. Worth touching. Worth empowering. She was worth it. All people are.

Jesus empowered this nameless woman and in so doing I was empowered. Like many women, I realized that Jesus' relationship with women was one of empowerment, and this relationship emboldened me to accept my call to ministry and recognize that Jesus was one of feminism's greatest allies. The responsibility of Christians is to walk in the footsteps of Jesus and empower those who are silenced, oppressed, and marginalized in our own society.

And such empowerment is happening at this very moment in an unexpected, subverted, yet incredibly powerful way. In fact, at the exact moment we gathered for worship his morning (10:30am), thousands of people from the Bay Area, the state of California, and likely the world, gathered on Market Street in San Francisco for the 39th annual Pride Parade. This weekend is the Lesbian, Gay, Bisexual, Transgender Pride Celebration.

I'm sure that you're familiar with Pride since both its good and bad stereotypes cover our television screens, magazines, and newspapers throughout this weekend and month of June. For some, Pride brings to mind bright, rainbow colors, feather boas, leather, people who are "different," and lewd and licentious behavior—something "Christians" should never be a part of. It's true that these things are, indeed, part of the Pride celebration. For others, Pride brings to mind bright, rainbow colors, the denial of rights to some of God's children, and the 1969 March on Stonewall, a protest against discrimination and violence against gays in New York City—something "Christians" should *certainly* be a part of.

I'll admit that when I learned that I would be preaching this Sunday, I wondered whether or not Pride would be something I should mention in my sermon. I thought about theologian Karl Barth's admonition that a preacher should prepare a sermon with a bible in one hand and a newspaper in the other. So, rather than ducking my head in the sand and ignoring what is going on in the world, I decided, perhaps I'll mention Pride. And then, also following Barth's admonition, I looked up the lectionary texts for today. 2 Samuel 1 and Mark 5. When I discovered that these were the texts for the day, I actually laughed out loud. "You've got to be kidding me?!" I thought. "Jonathan's love to David was wonderful, passing the love of women." You mean to tell me, oh-wise-lectionary-used-by-Christians-all-over-the-world, that the text for Pride Sunday is the text that overtly tells of David and Jonathan's loving relationship, the second story that shook my faith and theology to the core?

Then I decided, "forget about Pride for a moment," Angela. And just preach from the texts. "Jonathan's love to David was wonderful, passing the love of women." Now, many biblical scholars of a more conservative stripe have gone to great lengths with the David and Jonathan narratives to prove that these men were best friends, like brothers. David was married to Michal, or was it Bathsheba, or was it both, after all. David was described as a "man after God's own heart," despite his rock hurling at Goliath, rooftop spying on Bathsheba, murder of her husband Uriah, dancing and exposing himself in front of the arc of the covenant. Could it be that brave King David, the man after God's heart, was in love with Jonathan? I'd say that the text indicates so, especially when you read the rest of the David and Jonathan narratives from 1 Samuel. These texts tell us that "David became one in spirit with Jonathan and he loved him as himself," much like the two becoming one in Genesis. David and Jonathan later kiss and share clothing.

And if you're anything like I was the first time I translated these passages from Hebrew, you're probably thinking, "Enough is enough. Now is not the time or the place...church, worship, is not the forum to discuss such a relationship between two men: loving and becoming one in spirit and kissing and sharing clothing and surpassing love for women. Inappropriate …even if we read of it in our bible!"

If you're feeling that way, let me say that I understand. When the "church" has always told you that the bible is adamantly against homosexuality, that it's an abomination against God, then I would imagine that such an interpretation of the text could be jarring. It certainly was for me the first time I encountered it this way. When I sat next to Randall Bailey, a leading Hebrew Bible scholar and ordained Baptist minister, with my Hebrew bible open, pencil in hand, and tears streaming down my cheeks, I was quite shocked to translate this text. "Jonathan's love to David was wonderful, passing the love of women." This text, my translation, did not fit into the close-minded version of Christianity that had been handed to me. Every Christian I'd ever known told me that God hates gays. Dr. Randall Bailey told me that God loves all God's children, no matter their sexual orientation.

So, after reading these texts from the bible and after experiencing homophobia primarily from Christians who purport that the bible is unequivocally against homosexuality, how could I *not* speak of Pride this morning?

"Yes," many of you could be thinking, "of course, but we're a 'welcoming and affirming' congregation. We clearly don't think that God hates LGBTQ persons!" You're right. And I'm incredibly proud to serve as a pastor here. I'm honored to minister alongside an amazing group of Christians who are committed to justice and peace for *all* God's children. At the same time, many of us have expressed concern that we want to "open the door to the closet a little wider;" we've voted to officially be "welcoming and affirming," but now what?

Well, according to the Human Rights Campaign, there is no dearth of issues for which we can stand. When LGBTQ citizens can be fired on the basis of their sexual orientation without any legal recourse in thirty states, then we have a responsibility to say "enough is enough." When the United States does not allow same-sex couples the same immigration rights as heterosexual couples, we have a responsibility to say "enough is enough." When only ten states allow same-sex couples to jointly file for adoption of a child, we have a responsibility to say "enough is enough." When only six states allow same-sex marriages and twenty-nine states have passed state-wide constitutional amendments banning gay marriage, thus denying couples over one thousand federal protections granted to heterosexuals, we have a responsibility to say "enough is enough." When only thirteen states have laws that prohibit bullying, discrimination, or harassment in public schools against LGBTQ students, we have a responsibility to say "enough is enough."

It's no small thing to boldly proclaim, as Christians and as Baptists, that we are a welcoming and affirming congregation. Can we also take it one step further and *do* something about these injustices that afflict the LGBTQ community? And before we propose that these statistics are just numbers, or that they are small injustices that don't compare with the plight of global warming, poverty, or the need for healthcare, imagine for a moment that you were the parent of the Atlanta middle schooler that committed suicide only months ago because of gay bashing at his school. Imagine for a moment that you are deeply in love and have shared your entire life with your partner, and that partner is sick and dying in the hospital and you are denied the right to visit because the state doesn't consider you "family." Imagine for a moment that, in this time of economic crisis, you are fired from your job simply because you're gay. These are no small injustices that we're talking about here. What can we do to say "enough is enough?"

In our time and context of Pride Parades and oppression, this text from 2 Samuel isn't simply a trite love story between David and Jonathan. It's a blatant cry to all those "Christians" who told me or you or anyone that God doesn't love gay people to stop hating and start loving. The story of David and Jonathan, I would propose, is a perfect theme text for Pride. Because the entire point behind the concept of Pride is to empower and embolden those who have been silenced and told that they are unworthy, unloved, and damned to hell. The story of David's love for Jonathan can tell persons in the LGBTQ community that they are worthwhile, loved, and that their deep love for another is not only valued by God, but commended.

This story of David and Jonathan, like the story about our nameless woman, can serve as a paradigm for the voices of so many that have been silenced. Who are we silencing? Whose voice goes unheard in our society, in our church, in our own homes? And what are we going to do about it? Amen.

Conclusion

Hate mail, the misuse of scripture, the history of welcoming and affirming churches, queer understandings of the incarnation, queering liturgy, and Pride sermons combine to inform our understanding of how to gender the pulpit toward justice, inclusion, and radical welcome. You see, when I step into the pulpit to preach, I cannot take off my sexual identity. It is a part of who I am. It informs my understanding of experience, scripture, history, theology, and liturgy. My sexuality constructs the sermon and the sermon helps construct my sexual identity. When we allow our full identity—gendered, sexualized, and racialized—to enter into the pulpit with us, I am convinced that we gender the pulpit in the direction of radical hospitality. Because our sexualized bodies—aching, ageing, growing, desiring, dancing, fleshly bodies—preach on our behalf before we proclaim a single word.

Part II
Chapter 5
The Body and Gendered Pulpit

And all flesh shall see the salvation of God.
-Luke 3:6

WHEN PREPARING FOR THE INCARNATION, the writer of Luke quotes the prophet Isaiah, claiming that the incarnation will lead to a time when all flesh shall see the salvation of God. All *flesh* shall see the salvation of God. Not all hearts shall see the salvation of God. Not all minds. All flesh. This is an interesting choice of words for a variety of reasons. First, John the Baptist is preparing the way for God to be made flesh, for incarnation. All flesh shall see the salvation of God. Not in abstract, not in theory, but we shall actually see a fleshly living God born as a humble and needy baby just like you and me, with flesh and bones and tears and aches and pains and skin, flesh, hands, feet, a face. Just like us: a fleshly baby who is birthed from a fleshly womb that rips and tears and makes a big mess of divinity in a stinky manger. All flesh—breaking, stretching, birthing flesh—shall see the salvation of God.

And it's interesting that John proclaims that all flesh shall see the salvation of God as he prepares the way for God in flesh, but also because of what this word means. In Greek, flesh, here is *sarx* which literally means "flesh, physical body; human nature, earthly descent." Those things, those parts of you that you thought you had to overcome—your bodily realities— will see the salvation of God. Not just your heart. Not just your mind. Not just the squeaky clean parts of you. Your flesh, all flesh, all physical bodies, all human nature—even the parts that you don't like—shall see the salvation of God. All flesh. All physical bodies. All human nature. All earthly descent. All flesh shall see the salvation of God. Incarnational theology. Flesh that is born in a manger. Flesh in need of redemption. All flesh shall see the salvation of God.

The flesh doesn't really have the best reputation in Christianity, does it? The church has told us—primarily celibate men in power, I might add—that the flesh is secondary. The spirit is most important and the flesh is something to be overcome, negated, denied. This is why many Christians throughout the ages have denied their bodies, starved themselves, lacerated their skin, impaled their flesh in order to identify spiritually with the suffering of Christ. The bodies of those lacking power always had it the worst. For example, in the ancient world, the male body was the standard for beauty and desire, relegating women's bodies to a substandard not-quite-man and not-quite-beast. According to the Rabbinic Tosefta, men would pray: "Blessed who did not make me a gentile. Blessed who did not make me a woman. Blessed who did not make me a boar." Women's bodies were seen as deviant, as ancient scientists cited menstruation, breasts, womb, and lack of body hair to define female bodies as inferior to those of men.[77] Because they lacked a penis, Aristotle viewed women as deformed men.[78] As discussed throughout Part I of this book, queer bodies continue to be relegated to a secondary status, forced into constructed binaries of gender and sexuality. So, when the preacher's gendered and sexualized body steps into the pulpit, it carries with it centuries of baggage and shame. Yet, our bodies stand in the pulpit and proclaim that all flesh shall see the salvation of God.

Flesh gets dry and flakey, itchy, sweaty, it has rashes and bumps and bruises and scabs and cuts and scrapes. Flesh ages and stretches and grows and sags. Flesh can be oh-so-beautiful, sensuous, dripping with desire. And flesh can make you turn away your eyes in disgust. *All* that flesh shall see the salvation of God. The flesh and bodies that are bombed,

---

[77] Lesley Dean-Jones, "The Cultural Construct of the Female Body in Classical Greek Science," in *Women's History and Ancient History*, ed. Sarah Pomeroy (Chapel Hill: University of North Carolina Press, 1991): 111-137.
[78] Aristotle, *Generations of Animals* 737a25.

violated, seeking refuge, or spread across the covers of magazines as objects of desire. All that flesh, all those bodies shall see the salvation of God. All flesh. The flesh denied and the flesh affirmed. The flesh negated and the flesh celebrated. The flesh exploited and the flesh hidden. The flesh in power and the flesh oppressed by those in power. It is into this world—this world of juxtaposition and power imbalance—that God enfleshes God's self in the person of Jesus. In the womb of an unwed teenage mother, the most oppressed and denied flesh one could find, a baby God begins to form, floating in the amniotic fluid of holiness until the waiting ends and new life and love and hope spills out into the world.

The Christian tradition hinges in the flesh, the body, the incarnation. Without it there is no Jesus, no manger, no birth, no God-dwelling-among-us, no salvation. Without it, there is no good news, no Gospel. Without the incarnation, the preacher's body has nothing to proclaim. Marcia Mount Shoop reminds us of the importance of the body, saying, "Incarnation tells us that human flourishing is tied to an embodied fullness of life…In a disembodied faith, bodies languish, they are ignored, and they are silenced. As our bodies languish, so suffers everything about us—our spirits, minds, and emotions. In a re-embodied faith, bodies flourish, they are attended to, and they are heard."[79]

Part II of this book is rooted in an incarnational theology that values the body. In the pages that follow, we focus on the preacher's body and how the body proclaims in the Word in an embodied way. Homiletics scholar Teresa Fry Brown defines embodiment as "the act of representing something in a bodily or material form. It occurs when someone speaking uses their physical self to transform an abstract, mental idea into a concrete form, shape, or representation in order to assist in establishing its meaning for the audience."[80] In the act of preaching, Richard Wards calls this "body thinking."[81] What happens to the

---

[79] Shoop, 26.

[80] Teresa Fry Brown, *Delivering the Sermon* (Minneapolis: Fortress Press, 2008), 60.

[81] Richard Ward, *Speaking of the Holy* (St. Louis: Chalice Press, 2001), 38-39.

preaching event when we allow our bodies to do the thinking? How can our gendered and sexualized bodies gender the pulpit in the direction of justice?

I aim to respond to these questions by exploring the way the body has been affirmed and denied in the Christian tradition. By means of structure, I claim that one primary way the body has been affirmed is through dance in worship. So, chapter six focuses on dance in preaching and worship. Beginning with a story from personal experience, I delve into the theoretical underpinnings of dance in scripture, history, theology, and in theories of preaching and worship. I conclude the dance chapter with two practical examples for how to gender the pulpit by affirming the body with liturgical elements and a sermon. In chapter seven I claim that one primary way the body has gone awry in the Christian tradition is through eating disorders. So, chapter seven focuses on the role of eating disorders in preaching and worship. Here, a personal story is also the entry point into the theoretical underpinnings of eating disorders in scripture, history, theology, and theories of preaching and worship. As in every chapter, I conclude by offering two practical examples of addressing disordering eating in preaching and worship: liturgical elements and a sermon.

In order for the preacher to gender the pulpit in the direction of justice, in order for all flesh to see the salvation of God, we must acknowledge and take responsibility for the ways the body has gone awry in our tradition. At the same time, we must also celebrate the way the body has been and continues to be affirmed in preaching in worship.

Chapter 6

The Body Affirmed: Preaching, Worship, and Dance

A QUINTESSENTIAL BAPTIST JOKE ABOUT DANCE goes a little something like this. A Baptist seminary professor is walking through campus when he (of course the professor is male in the joke) happens upon a couple rustling around in the bushes. He confronts the couple and asks, "What are you doing there in those bushes?!" The couple blushes and responds, "Why, we're having sex, professor." "Good," the weary professor balks, "I was worried you were dancing!" Admonitions such as this one make preachers wonder, "Can the body be affirmed through dance?"

In determining how to more fully celebrate and honor the body in preaching and worship, I examine scripture, history, theology, and theories in preaching and worship. My starting point, however, is personal experience. As a professional dancer who has dedicated much of my ministry and research to the intersections of dance and religion, there are plenty of dancing stories I could share. I've found that dance is most evocative and meaningful, however, when it empowers those who have previously never used their bodies as a conduit for worship, or whose gender or sexuality has been excluded from worship leadership. So, I begin with the story of twenty-two dancers in a small Southern town.

Embodied Hallelujahs

The scene is a small town in South Georgia. It's Easter Sunday and a Baptist church gathers together for worship in the large conference room of a hotel. The church had recently split off from a Southern Baptist Convention due in part to this community's desire to ordain women and their progressive approach to scripture and theology. Until they could raise the funds to build a sanctuary, they worshipped in this conference room. I was their youth and children's minister and this was our first Easter as a newly formed community of faith.

After silencing our Hallelujahs throughout the season of Lent—and during a painful church split—our voices and spirits were raised that Easter morning as twenty-two women and girls gathered in back of the space. Clad in white skirts, girls as young as three, grandmothers, and a variety of ages in-between stretched their hearts and bodies. A few in the congregation were a little worried. "Dancing on Easter Sunday?! What if there are visitors? Our new church already has a reputation for being open-minded. What will people think when they hear that we danced down the aisles to celebrate resurrection?" Our pastor assured these concerned congregants that all would be well, that I had it under control, and that dance is, indeed, embedded in our history.

I was a twenty-one year-old college senior who had ministered among these beloved people for nearly four years. Together we laughed, cried, traveled, sang, and formed a new community based on equality, love, and acceptance. And in that hotel conference room in a small South Georgia town, we danced. Harmonized and robust *Hallelujahs* filled the room as the youngest ones in our group began twirling up the aisle. Soon, our elementary school aged girls joined them, followed by some of our teenagers who had dance training, their choreography more complex than that of the younger ones. Soon, some of our mothers and younger women joined. As the *Hallelujahs* grew louder and stronger, two women in walkers made their way up the aisle. Shuffle. Shuffle. Scoot the walker. Raise an arm. Shuffle. Shuffle. Scoot the walker. Raise the other arm.

For weeks they rehearsed. Women who were raised in a faith tradition that told them that dance was a sin and a culture that called dancing girls loose and wanton. Women who were always told that their bodies were objects of shame and that their gender excluded them from possibilities of ordained ministry.

Those same women leapt up and down the aisles that Easter Sunday morning. They danced. They were deemed ministers. They celebrated resurrection with their bodies. And their daughters danced, too. Without the stigma associated with dancing in worship, without being told that their gender excluded them from worship leadership, these young girls danced.

I wish I could describe the empowerment and affirmation these myriad bodies felt that Easter Sunday morning. These dancing little girls will grow up without all the taboo and stigma associated with their gendered bodies that their mothers experienced. And their mothers and grandmothers joined them in the dance, their bodies affirmed for the first time in their lives in the context of worship. Dancing ministers, I called them.

On Easter Sunday, the Christian tradition reminds us that Jesus found the body so important that he took it with him. The body was resurrected, too. As a progressive person of faith, I often find myself struggling to explain the resurrection of the body from the pulpit. I am convinced, however, that the body of Christ is resurrected in each of us, in our dancing bodies. So, it was fitting that we danced that Easter Sunday morning. It was fitting that we became resurrection with our dancing bodies. Whenever I hear of churches that forsake their dancing history—the history I will soon expound upon—I think back to that Easter Sunday morning. In the most conservative place I have ever lived, in a Baptist church, as senior adults joined with young children, a community embodied what it means to worship. Women's bodies were affirmed. The community was redeemed. Our Hallelujahs embodied the bodily resurrection. It was surely an Easter Sunday I will not soon forget.

Scripture and Dance

Praise God's name with dancing.
-Psalm 149:3

Before we even read of "dance" in scripture, we find embodied words for worship and praise filling both testaments. First, we read the Hebrew word y*adah* over seventy times in the Hebrew bible; it is translated as "praise," but literally means "to confess with outstretched hands." Second, we read another word translated as "praise," *barak*, which literally means, "to kneel, bless, praise." In other words, every time the word "praise" is read, the word literally has an embodied connotation, either outstretching the hands or kneeling. Even more fascinating is the Hebrew word for worship, s*hachah*. This word is translated as "worship" over one-hundred and seventy times in the Hebrew bible, but it literally means, "to prostrate, bow down, do reverence to." Furthermore, this Hebrew word is a Hishtaphel[82] reflexive, which means it is an act that is reciprocated; every time an individual *shachahs* to God, God *shachahs* in return. As you bow to God, God bows to you. Worship and praise, in the Hebrew Bible, are kinesthetic in nature. So, for the ancient Israelites, the notions of worship and praise were not activities that occurred in the mind or heart alone, but instead infiltrated the entire body. Worship was an embodiment of faith. The body was affirmed as a vital part of worship.

In addition to worship and praise existing as embodied, there are ten Hebrew verb forms for the one word "dance" used throughout the Hebrew bible: r*ekad, pazez, mahol, gul, chagag, kirker, dillug, chul, sabab, pasah, siheq*.[83] Ten different words were used to describe our one English word for "dance." This concept seems similar to the way that Eskimos have so many words to describe snow; they need a variety of words to describe snow because it is so prevalent in their daily lives and culture. Dance was so ingrained in the culture and worship of the ancient Israelites that they needed over ten verb forms to describe it. The ancient Israelites—our worshipping ancestors—were an embodied people, dancing in the grips of God's joy and dancing in the face lament or oppression.

Also in the Christian canon, we discover that dance and movement are embedded in the Greek text. Primarily, the Greek

---

[82] Some scholars also assert that *shachah* is actually a Hithpael reflexive rather than a Hishtaphel reflexive. The debate between these two camps is beyond the scope of this study as the importance of the term is that it is reflexive and, therefore, reciprocated.

[83] Mayer Gruber, "Ten Dance-Derived Expressions in the Hebrew Bible," in *Dance as Religious Studies*, ed. Doug Adams and Diane Apostolos-Cappadona (New York: Crossroads Publishing Company, 1990): 48-66.

word, *aggallio,* literally means "very much leaping/jump for joy," but is translated as "exceedingly glad or joyful" over fifteen times in the New Testament. When "joy" is read, therefore, dancing is understood, for rejoicing and dancing are synonymous.[84] Furthermore, the Greek word translated as "worship" over fifty times, p*roskunaeo,* literally means, "to worship, fall down, kneel, bow low, fall at another's feet." The words for worship were embodied in nature in the same manner that they are in the Hebrew Bible. Accordingly, the body continued to be valued as a conduit for worship in the New Testament.

What is more, there are a variety of stories about dancers in scripture.[85] In Exodus Miriam dances on the shores of freedom after crossing the Sea of Reeds. Upon their escape from slavery, Miriam and the other Israelites chose to celebrate their liberation with dance and song, their bodies affirmed and free. In Judges, Jephthah's daughter dances out the doors of her house to greet her father upon his return from battle. Such a greeting was traditional and expected by women and girls in ancient Israelite culture upon the return of men from battle. Yet, Jephthah's daughter's dance morphs from a dance of greeting to a dance of lamentation as her father sacrifices her because of his foolish vow. In these ways, dance in scripture functions in both celebration and lament. So, too, do we see dances of wild abandon. 2 Samuel recounts the way King David danced as the Ark of the Covenant was delivered into his city, leaping wildly and exposing his glory to everyone gathered. With both decency and propriety thrown to the wind, David danced in the grips of God's unabashed love. Similarly, the Shulamite dances in the grips of unabashed love. Only the Shulamite's dance is before the eyes of her beloved who dotes upon her every curve in Song of Songs. Her sensuous dance teaches worshipers of the

---

[84] Margaret Taylor, "A History of Symbolic Movement in Worship," in *Dance as Religious Studies*, ed. Doug Adams and Diane Apostolos-Cappadona (New York: Crossroads Publishing Company, 1990), 16.

[85] For a detailed analysis of dance in scripture and how it impacts worship, see Angela Yarber, *Dance in Scripture: How Biblical Dancers Can Revolutionize Worship Today* (Eugene: Wipf and Stock, 2013).

importance of passionate love. In the book of Judith, the woman for whom the book is named dances with all the women after defeating the enemy and chopping off the head of her oppressor. Her beautiful body, faithful heart, and wise mind combine subversively so that her dance undermines a male custom and instead empowers women to affirm their bodies as agents of worship, victory, and liberation. In Matthew and Mark a little girl dances to the delight of her father who then beheads John the Baptist. The innocent young child is later named Salome and her dance is demonized throughout history as one that leads to death and wanton seduction. Yet, the text describes the dancing dalliances of a little girl who plays, leaps, and skips like many young children when given the spotlight. And the Apocryphal Acts of John describe the dance of Jesus, who gathers in a circle to sing a hymn with his disciples and proclaims, "Grace dances, dance ye all…the number twelve dance on high…all on high have part in our dance…those who dance not, know not what is to come."

Throughout scripture, dance is admonished as a form of praise, as evidenced by Psalm 149 and 150, along with Ecclesiastes 3. And these diverse dancing figures—Miriam, Jephthah's daughter, David, the Shulamite, Judith, Salome, and Jesus—remind us of the primacy of the body in worship. Dance is seen as a way to express liberation and celebration, while also functioning as a form of lament. Abandon and passionate love are invoked through worshipful dances. Subversion and innocence are embodied by these scriptural dancers. And Jesus' dance teaches worshipers of the power of community to gather hand-in-hand, celebrating and honoring the bodies within the circle and beyond.

How might the pulpit be gendered differently if preachers proclaimed the power of these texts that affirm and celebrate the body? It's worth noting how infrequently these dancing texts appear in the Revised Common Lectionary. The dances of David, Miriam, and Salome are in the lectionary, but the dances Jephthah's daughter, the Shulamite, Judith, and Jesus are never listed. Would the proclamation of the Word look and feel differently if gendered bodies danced the Word in addition to speaking it? Is proclamation limited only to disembodied voices? It is clear that scripture teaches us that dance and the body are primary when it comes to worship and preaching. So, too, does the history of the Christian tradition.

History of Dance in Christianity

The examples of dance in scripture are illustrative of the prominent role of the body and dance in early Christian worship. Additionally, many of the early church "fathers"[86] speak of dance as a form of worship in their writings. Rather than elaborating upon each of their writings, I will simply allow their brief statements to serve as representations of the prevalence of dance in the early church.[87] For example, Lucian of Samosata (125-180) stated, "Dance is not merely a pleasure; it is an act good for the soul."[88] Clement of Alexandria (150-216) in his *Address to the Heathens*, said, "This is the mountain beloved of God…and there revel on it…daughters of God, the fair lambs, who celebrate the holy rites of the Word, raising a sober choral dance."[89] Furthermore, Ambrose (338-397) requested that persons about to be baptized approach the font dancing.[90] And Hippolytus's (170-236) Easter hymn of praise sings, "O thou leader of the mystic round dance" when referring to God.[91] Eusebius of Caesarea (264?-339) speaks of dance as worship

[86] I would surmise that many early church "mothers" likely supported dance in worship, but since they existed in a time of patriarchy, their voices and possible writings were not preserved or viewed as valuable.

[87] By no means to do I think that dance in worship was the primary concern of every church father who mentions dance in writings; however, the confines of this book limit the amount of space I can dedicate to the role of dance in the early church. I do think that the sheer number of references to dance likely speaks to the frequency of dance in the Christian church during this time.

[88] Ronald Gagne, Thomas Kane, and Robert VerEecke, *Introducing Dance in Christian Worship* (Portland: Pastoral Press, 1999), 30.

[89] Roberts, *The Ante-Nicene Fathers*, as quoted in Gagne, Kane, and VerEecke, 30.

[90] Ambrose, "On Repentance," as quoted in Gagne, Kane, and VerEecke, 31.

[91] Hippolytus, *Homily in Pascha* as quoted in Gagne, Kane, and VerEecke, 31.

when he says, "With dances and hymns, in city and country, they glorified first of all God the universal King."[92] Even Jerome (340-407), one who is known for disdaining the body, stated, "In the Church the joy of the spirit finds expression in bodily gestures and her children shall say with David as they dance the solemn step: 'I will dance and play before the face of the Lord.'"[93] What is more, Basil the Great (344-407) described dance in the church beautifully when he writes, "We remember those who now, together with the Angels, dance the dance of the Angels around God, just as in the heavenly dance...Could there be anything more blessed than to imitate on earth the ring-dance of the angels and at dawn to raise our voices in prayer and by hymns and song glorify the rising Creator."[94] Additionally, in Gregory of Nyssa's *Homily on the Psalms* he writes, "Once there was a time when the whole of rational creation formed a single dancing chorus looking upwards to the one leader of this dance. And the harmony of that motion which was imparted to them by reason of his [sic] law found its way into their dancing."[95] And even Augustine (354-430), a theologian responsible for shaping much of Christianity, spoke of the relationship between dance and faith, writing, "He [sic] who dances obeys...In our case dancing means changing the manner of our life...when God called the tune, he [sic] hearkened and began to dance."[96] These early church fathers are generally not remembered as ones who celebrated and affirmed the body. Further, their reputations often involve diminishing the role of women. How might their writings on dance subvert their otherwise patriarchal reputations? Would preaching and worship look differently if we emphasized the danced writings of these early church fathers as much as we emphasized their writings on sin, atonement, and salvation? Could highlighting their writings on dance—an embodied affirmation of the flesh—gender worship and the pulpit differently?

---

[92] Gagne, Kane, and VerEecke, 37.
[93] Gagne, Kane, and VerEecke, 39.
[94] Iris Stewart, *Sacred Woman Sacred Dance* (Rochester: Inner Traditions, 2000), 64.
[95] Gagne, Kane, and VerEecke, 41.
[96] Gagne, Kane, and VerEecke, 41.

Not only did the early church support dance as worship, but it continued into the Early Medieval period. During this time ecclesiastical censures of dance begin, indicating perhaps that dance in worship was prevalent and those in power did not like the equality it brought between clergy and laity. The Council of Toledo in 589 curtailed excesses by trying to limit dance in worship to saints' days, also indicating that dance was otherwise prevalent during worship on a regular basis.[97] One example of sacred dance during this time was the Festival of Fools before Lent, which was filled with singing, dancing, and feasting in churches and was eventually baptized into the Feast of Circumcision or Epiphany. Additionally, the Archbishop Isidore of Seville composed sacred choreography and incorporated it into the Mozarabic Rite that is still celebrated three times per year in the Cathedral of Seville.[98] Another example is that Pope Gregory IV (827-844) inaugurated the Children's Festival in honor of Pope Gregory the Great where children danced in worship.[99]

Continuing into the Late Medieval Period (1100-1400), which is described as the age of dramatic expression as mass takes the form of the mystery play. The most prominent form of dance during this time is the Dance of Death, "danse macabre," where death dances forth to claim the lives of those stricken with the Bubonic Plague.[100] Also during the Late Medieval Period, cloistered nuns danced on the Feasts of Holy Innocents, priests danced on the Feast of St. Nicholas, Pope Urban IV (1264) created the Corpus Christi procession dance to celebrate the Eucharist, and labyrinth dances were popular in church-yards.[101] A dance step that has continued until today—the oldest liturgical dance step—stems from the work of John Beleth, the University of Paris rector, who inaugurated the tripudia.[102] And it is during

---

[97] Taylor, 19.
[98] Taylor, 19.
[99] Gagne, Kane, and VerEecke, 43.
[100] Taylor, 23.
[101] Gagne, Kane, VerEecke, 46.
[102] The tripudia is traditionally used in processionals and involves stepping forward with the right foot, then stepping forward with the left

this period that Dante describes dancing as "the occupation of those in paradise."[103]

We move from the Late Medieval Period into the Renaissance (1400-1700), where processionals, moral ballets, and dance as hymn and psalm interpretation are prevalent in worship. Cardinal Ximenes (1436-1517) choreographed "seises" dances to be performed seven time per year, and Pope Eugenius IV saw these seises and issued a papal bull authorizing their dances.[104] Beginning the Protestant tradition, Martin Luther, admonishes dance in his 1525 carol "On Heaven High" in addition to writing about it in a letter to his little son, Hans, describing heaven as a place of happy dancing. Furthermore, Luther writes about dance in a sermon for Epiphany II:

> …because it is the custom of the country, just like inviting guests, dressing up, eating, drinking, and making merry, I can't bring myself to condemn it, unless it gets out of hand, and so causes immoralities or excess. And even though sin has taken place in this way, it's not the fault of dancing alone. Provided they don't jump on tables dancing in the church…But so long as it's done decently, I respect the rights and customs of weddings—and *I* dance, anyway![105]

Additionally, Cardinal Borromeo, commissioned a dance for the canonization of Ignatius of Loyola in 1610.[106] In 1588 Thoinot Arbeau wrote defense of religious dancing and in 1682 Menestriere, a Jesuit priest from Paris, spoke of dance being used in the Divine Office.[107] And as the Renaissance draws to a

---

foot, then stepping once again with the right foot, and then shifting the weight back onto the left foot and repeating the steps over and over.

[103] Canto VII lines 7-9 in Dante Alighieri, *Paradiso*, trans. John Ciardi (New York: New American Library, 1997), 62.

[104] Gagne, Kane, and VerEecke, 49.

[105] This sermon appeared in a pamphlet entitled, "The Difference Between True and False Worship," Martin Luther, 1522 available at http://www.godrules.net/library/luther/129luther_a12.htm [accessed December 1, 2008].

[106] Taylor, 28.

[107] Taylor, 28.

close, the Council of Trent (1545-1563) condemned dance, even though it ended with a lavish ball.[108]

During the Post Renaissance, the Jesuits stylized the famous five positions of ballet under the leadership of Charles Beauchamp, and the Jesuit's college ballets could be compared to the court ballets of their day. In fact, King Louis XIV once said, "there is no one like the Jesuits for doing pirouettes."[109] On the whole there was a decline in liturgical dancing due to the shift toward word-oriented liturgy, as the Roman Catholic Church became more centrally authoritative, and Puritans condemned the lust of the flesh; however, John Cotton, a New England Puritan, stated, "Dancing I would not simply condemn, for I see two sorts of dancing in use with God's people in the OT."[110] Cotton Mather, another Puritan, wrote "An Arrow Against Profane and Promiscuous Dancing," and condemned only dancing that aroused the passions.[111] Furthermore, the Shakers, founded 1747, were known for their unique, shaking dances in worship.[112] There were circle dances in camp meetings of Baptists, Methodists, and Presbyterians during the Second Great Awakening.

And dance was surely present in the worship of Christians outside of European-American history, but colonialism manifested in the form of Western missionaries managed to snuff out the majority of its record. We catch glimpses of dance in worship from African traditions when Africans are forced into slavery in the United States and form brush/hush harbors where they dance the "ring shout" in secret worship services hidden in the woods.[113] Although there are a

---

[108] Gagne, Kane, and VerEecke, 49.

[109] Judith Rock, *Terpsichore at Louis-le-Grand: Baroque Dance on the Jesuit Stage in Paris* (Saint Louis: The Institute of Jesuit Sources, 1996), 39.

[110] Taylor, 29.

[111] Taylor, 29.

[112] Taylor, 30.

[113] For more details regarding the role of the ring shout and dance in African American worship, see Art Rosenbaum, *Shout Because You're Free: The African American Ring Shout Tradition in Coastal Georgia* (Athens: University of Georgia Press, 1998), Albert J. Raboteau, *Slave*

great deal of variations, Michael Gomez notes that the ring shout often involves gathering into a circle to dance counterclockwise in a manner that evokes spiritual unity.[114] According to Lawrence Levine, slaves use the ring shout as an "outlet for the physical and spiritual passions as well as a bridge to the thin line between past and present."[115] In some cases, slaves retreated into the woods at night to perform shouts, often for hours at a time, with participants leaving the circle as they became exhausted. A poignant example of such a ring shout is evidenced in Toni Morrison's *Beloved* as Baby Suggs, Holy, preaches and dances a powerful sermon on behalf of her enslaved community:

> It started that way: laughing children, dancing men, crying women and then it got mixed up. Women stopped crying and danced; men sat down and cried; children danced, women laughed, children cried until, *exhausted and riven*, all and each lay about the Clearing damp and gasping for breath. In the silence that followed, Baby Suggs, holy, offered up to them her great big heart.[116]

She goes on to remind all the broken, beaten, oppressed bodies gathered of the way their flesh is treated by their white masters, but how their duty is to love their flesh, "love it, love it hard." In the holy space that is the clearing, Baby Suggs finishes the spoken word and continues to "dance with her twisted hip the rest of what her heart had to say while the others opened their

---

Religion: The "Invisible Institution" in the Antebellum South (New York: Oxford University Press, 1978) or Samuel Floyd, "Ring Shout! Literary Studies, Historical Studies, and Black Music Inquiry," in *Black Music Research Journal,* Vol. 22 (2002).

[114] Michael Gomez, *Exchanging Our Country Masks* (Chapel Hill: University of North Carolina Press, 1998), 244-63.

[115] Lawrence Levine, *Black Culture and Black Consciousness* (Oxford: Oxford University Press, 1977), 165.

[116] Toni Morrison, *Beloved* (New York: Penguin Group, 1987), 88-89. *Italics mine.*

mouths and gave her the music. Long notes held until the four part harmony was perfect enough for their deeply loved flesh."[117] It is worth noting that the sermon—the spoken word—was not perfect enough. Rather, it was the singing and dancing body that provided liberation, that brought about the realization that flesh was deeply loved. Surely the Invisible Institution of slave worship was filled with dances of liberation that affirmed and honored the oppressed and marginalized body. In these ways, the gendered and racialized body proclaims the good news, proclaims salvific liberation.

And in modernity, the Second Vatican Council's *Constitution on the Sacred Liturgy, Sacrosanctum Consilium*, 1964, "gave back to the human body its freedom to praise its creator in many different ways."[118] Pentecostal and Charismatic worshippers participate in "dancing in the spirit." "Praise dance" is prevalent in some evangelical and many African American churches. And "Liturgical dance" is present in countless "liturgical" churches throughout the world. It is more than evident, in these brief examples throughout history, that dance has held a special place in worship throughout the history of the Christian church. Since Jesus proclaimed that "those who dance not know not,"[119] throughout history, and into the present, Christians dance as an embodiment of their faith, as a way to affirm the body.

Worship that moves, gestures, and dances affirms the body in ways that static worship simply cannot. Acknowledging the rich and deep history of dance in the Christian tradition is an imperative part of gendering worship and preaching. When we deny the body in worship, we forsake our history. When we neglect dance in worship and preaching, we act as though thousands of years of dancing history never occurred in the confines of Christian worship. Our dancing history empowers

---

[117] Morrison, 88-89.

[118] Carla DeSola, "Liturgical Dance: State of the Art," in *Postmodern Worship and the Arts*, ed. Doug Adams and Michael Moynahan (San Jose: Resource Publications, 2002), 96.

[119] Van der Leeuw, 29.

gendered bodies to join hearts and minds in the pulpit and in the pew. Rather than denying, forsaking, neglecting, or negating the body, we have the power to celebrate and honor the body in preaching and worship through dance. It is a dancing history that is in our bones and when we dance, our bodies join with the myriad dancers who have moved in the grips of God's liberating joy throughout our collective history. When our gendered bodies step into the pulpit, this dancing history is present, moving, breathing, and living within us. So, too, is the dance present in our theology.

Theology and Dance

One cannot end suffering except through dance.
-Alice Walker

I assume that when you think about theology, dance is not the first thing that comes to mind, or when you think about dance, theological insights don't immediately rush to the forefront of your imagination. Yet, not only is dance a vital method for grappling with esoteric theological concepts, it is actually present and inseparable from the very foundations of Christian theology. The theological concepts of Trinity, creation, incarnation, and community are inextricably linked with dance, and these four theological concepts dance together in a way that bolsters, sustains, and upholds the others, much like adagio dancers, who lift, glide, bend, and move together as a unit.

So, too, do the persons of the Trinity, a foundational concept in Christian theology. Early church father, John of Damascus, is responsible for most fully naming the Trinity as *Perichoresis*. *Perichoresis* is a Greek term that refers to the mutual coinherence and indwelling of this confusing three-in-one God. But the term *Perichoresis* actually comes from *perichoreo*, which literally means "to dance round," indicating that the communal relationship of the Trinity is that of a round dance. You cannot have a round dance with only one or two people; there must be at least three. Each member of the trinity—Creator, Redeemer, Sustainer—relies on the other in the round dance, hands held in community, illustrating reciprocity, give-and-take, permeating, indwelling, and mutual embrace. The Trinity, God as three-in-one, She Who Is, according to Elizabeth Johnson, is a dancing community. So, the very foundation of Christian theology, the Trinity, traditionally rendered Father-Son-Holy Spirit, relies on dance for its very existence. And this communal dance of the Trinity naturally gives way to three other theological concepts in Christianity: creation, incarnation and community.

In Genesis 1 we read that "in beginning, God created the heavens and the earth, the earth was a formless void and darkness covered the face of the deep." This word, deep, in Hebrew is *tehom*. *Tehom* translates as "deep or depths," but it is also a cognate for *Tiamat*. And *Tiamat* is the dancing Babylonian Goddess of creation, who essentially births the world into being. In the beginning was a dancing goddess who birthed the world into being; out of the deep, out of *Tiamat*, the earth is created. Further in the Genesis account, we read in 1:26 that the text says, "let *us* make humankind in *our* image," not let *me* make humankind in *my* image. Perhaps the *us* and *our* here is indicative of the communal dancing trinity, or perhaps it references God and *Tiamat* birthing the world from the dancing depths. Either way, dance is part of creation, the creation of the earth and the creation of humanity.

The body is not only affirmed and celebrated by the Trinity and creation, but also by the theological concept of incarnation. The theological concept of incarnation involves God enfleshing God's self in the person of Jesus. But Jesus does not simply drop out of the clouds in fleshly form as a grown adult. Rather, God incarnates God's self in the fleshly womb of an unwed teenage mother. Burgeoning in the amniotic fluid of holiness, forming flesh and fingernails, growing a heart and organs, baby Jesus is born just like you and me. Mary's womb is a space of holy becoming as it rips and tears divinity into being, spilling out a baby God into the stench of a manger. The body is real and needy. Our baby God burps and coos, cries and draws nourishment from the breast of his mother. Flesh upon flesh. Scripture recounts that the babies leap in their mothers' wombs. So, dancing occurs before Jesus even draws his first breath. The incarnation, like the Trinity, is a foundational part of the

Christian faith. It is not simply that Jesus had a body. Jesus was a body, a body that grew and ached, desired and suffered, bled and ate, drank and died. Jesus' body did the same things our bodies do. In these ways, the incarnation celebrates and honors the importance of the body from birth through death. In fact, Jesus found the body to be so important that he took it with him when he was resurrected. In the womb, in birth, and even in death, the body was primary. Incarnation is primary.

The more theoretical concepts of Trinity, creation, and incarnation lead to the practical theological concept of community. Womanist theologian Karen Baker Fletcher describes the way the dance of the trinity leads to community in her book, *Dancing with God*.[120] Baker Fletcher not only affirms and describes *Perichoresis*, or the dance of the Trinity, but she concludes that the communal dance of the Trinity urges us to create reciprocal, mutually embracing, welcoming, permeating communities. These communities are places where we join with those who are rejoicing *and* suffering by dancing hand-in-hand, in solidarity, equally, creating justice for all. Dancing justice for all. Dancing, wading, in the water so that all of humanity might move toward places of freedom and equality. Forming community is also a central tenant of the Christian faith. This is why we have churches and communal worship and the proclamation of the word. Faith can certainly be personal, but faith grows within the confines of community where bodies gather together for support, encouragement, and to be the hands and feet of God on earth. In these ways, the communal dancing of faith communities mirrors the dance of the trinity.

It is evident, therefore, that dance not only reflects theology, but theology also reflects dance. From the beginning of the creation narrative to the dance of the Trinity, from the incarnation of God in flesh to the flesh of Christian community, the body is affirmed, celebrated, and honored through dance. Dance is theological. The affirmation of the gendered body is theological. How might our corporate and individual theologies of the body shift if we embodied the theological concepts of

---

[120] Karen Baker Fletcher, *Dancing with God* (St. Louis: Chalice Press, 2006).

Trinity, creation, incarnation, and community? Would worship and preaching be gendered differently if we embodied Trinity, creation, incarnation, and community more frequently?

Preaching, Liturgy, and Dance

Scripture, history, and theology all find their way into the embodied practices of preaching and worship. Marcia Mount Shoop names the disembodied problem of most mainline Protestant churches when it comes to preaching in worship. Her concerns echo the need for dance and the affirmation of the body: "Our sermons speak of transformation and being Spirit-filled, but we are not sure how redemption relates to our flesh-and-blood bodies. Communion liturgy tells us we become the Body of Christ in the mystery of the Lord's Supper, and still we sit quietly and wonder what it all could mean for us."[121]

Of particular importance in addressing these concerns in relation to preaching is Judith Rock's notion of the performer being both a priest and prophet. And of particular importance in worship is the notion of communion and the Body of Christ. Judith Rock's book *Performer as Priest and Prophet* deals with how to restore the intuitive in worship through music and dance. Her understanding of what it means to be a performer is helpful when dealing with congregants who oppose dance because they feel it is a "performance." Rock explains that "perform," according to the Oxford English Dictionary, means "to carry through in due form, accomplishing entirely." She explains that "a performer 'carries through' by serving a form or craft, subordinating the self to it in order to communicate."[122] A dancer, like a preacher, must subordinate the self to the art of dancing and preaching, "serving choreographic and technical forms so that communication can take place through a disciplined, articulate body."[123] In these ways, dancing is not any different than preaching or singing in the choir when the performer submits the self to the craft of worship and

---

[121] Shoop, 123-24.

[122] Judith Rock and Norman Mealy, *Performer as Priest and Prophet* (San Francisco: Harper and Row Publishers, 1988), 79.

[123] Rock, 80.

proclaiming the Word. A preacher, like a dancer, is also a performer that requires requisite training, technique, preparation, research, and embodied expertise.

Rock continues by highlighting the importance of dancers—like preachers—being both priestly and prophetic. A priestly preacher and dancer consoles, guards, sanctions, and reminds the community of their place in history and tradition. A prophetic preacher and dancer challenges, judges, and reminds the community of their call to stand for justice, inclusion, and equality. Further, when the preacher proclaims the Word with the entire body instead of just the head, voice, and heart, the gathered community can see and feel how the body is affirmed, honored, and celebrated.

Consequently, preachers have much to learn from dancers and performers who train their bodies and voices so that they may be seen, heard, and understood by audiences. How many sermons have you heard where you wished the preacher had taken a class in acting and could shift and inflect the voice rather than sounding monotone? How many sermons have you seen where limbs are plastered to the preacher's side and the body is hidden behind a massive pulpit or inside a bulky robe? How might the Word be proclaimed differently if preachers moved and danced in a way that acknowledges the importance of the body? Could the proclamation of the Word liberate more freely and fully if the gendered body moved within the pulpit, honoring, celebrating, and affirming the body as a conduit for grace? What might happen if sermons were embodied with the entire body rather than merely spoken? What might happen if a sermon danced?

The notion of the body being a conduit for grace is essential in communion and the Body of Christ, as well. The Body of Christ is a complex double entendre riddled with symbolic and embodied meaning in the Christian tradition. On the one hand, the Body of Christ refers to precisely that: Christ's body. The body of Jesus: born in a manger, moving and healing and preaching and eating throughout a desert landscape, stripped, beaten, and crucified, left to die in the hollow of a hill, and resurrected with scarred hands and feet. Jesus had a body. Jesus was a body. It was the Body of Christ: gendered, aging, growing, desiring, aching, naked, suffering, dying, resurrected. On the other hand, the Body of Christ also refers to you and me. The Christian community is the Body of Christ, God's hands and feet in the world. According to many denominations, when one professes faith in Jesus, or becomes baptized, one becomes a part of the larger Body of Christ. This Body includes a myriad of bodies—young and old, sick and healthy, gendered, sexualized, and racialized in diverse ways, oppressed and objectified, beautiful and not so beautiful. All those bodies, from many years past through the present and from all over the globe, constitute the Body of Christ. So, the Body of Christ is the physical body of a person—or God—born in a body that was constructed and understood as male. And the Body of Christ is also a whole bunch of other bodies: male, female, transgender, queer, and questioning.

All of these understandings of the Body of Christ are present and real and lived and experienced and even eaten at the communion meal. Ministers break bread and dub it "the Body of Christ." And then we eat it. Chew it. Swallow it. Digest it. Excrete it. The Body of Christ makes its way through our bodies and our bodies are the Body of Christ. And the bread we consume symbolizes (or *is,* depending on your tradition) the Body of Christ. So, the Body of Christ is eaten and makes its way through the Body of Christ so that we can remember the Body of Christ. In the Gospel of John Jesus lays this out plainly, saying, "Eat my flesh and drink my blood." Shoop expounds on how removed the church has become from this fleshly and embodied concept:

> 'Eat my flesh and drink my blood' sounds bizarre, even inappropriate, to our refined ears. Making Jesus' words metaphorical tempers their jarring sound. Surely Jesus is not really talking about his flesh and blood, but some kind of spiritualized assent to who he was and is. That sounds more like something we can hear. The metaphor lets us keep our distance from the words themselves. And this metaphorical interpretation authorizes our perceptions of embodied distance from each other,

> from our own bodies, and from everything that lives and breathes.[124]

In my own tradition as a Baptist, and in countless other Protestant traditions, we try so hard to make sure that our Eucharistic theology is *not* Catholic. We claim that we are not actually eating the Body of Christ, but a symbol of it, a representation. And there are good theological and historical and existential reasons for these distinctions. But what does truncating the Body of Christ—the bread—to a mere symbol do for our own bodies? As Shoop contends, does not Jesus manifest this metaphor with his own body? According to John, Jesus desires to be inside of us and for us to be in him. Consequently, communion does not just remember what Jesus was and what he did. Eating the Body of Christ reminds us that Jesus had a body, that we have bodies, and that those bodies are joined together in the act of eating and drinking at communion. Remembering reconciles us to Christ, to one another, and to the land that produced the bounty we consume in the act of communion. "Remembering the Body of Christ means re-membering our bodies as redeemed by the Body of Christ, by the promise of God embodied."[125]

Our dancing, growing, aching, aging bodies are the Body of Christ. And these bodies are affirmed, celebrated, honored, reconciled, and even redeemed in the embodied act of consuming the Body of Christ. Preaching, worship, and communion merge in the dancing body. How might communion be understood differently if our bodies were understood as a real, reciprocated, living, and breathing part of the sacrament? How might our bodies be affirmed and celebrated if we looked in the mirror and, instead of seeing our faults and flaws, we saw the Body of Christ staring back at us? Our bodies perform our genders and embody our theologies in the pulpit and at the communion table. Our gendered bodies embody the Body of Christ in our preaching, our dancing, and our eating.

---

[124] Shoop, 165.
[125] Shoop, 169.

Practical Application: Sermon and Liturgy

Scripture, history, theology, and the theories of preaching and worship pave the way for the practical work of affirming the body through dance. On a rare occasion the Revised Common Lectionary does include a few texts that deal with dance. On these days, highlighting the way the body can be affirmed through dance is one way to help gender the pulpit in an embodied manner. Also, taking an opportunity to preach about other texts that deal with dance that are not included in the lectionary is important. Further, incorporating the affirmation of the body into regular worship is a key to gendering the pulpit and worship space in a way that celebrates the beauty and goodness of the body. In the pages that I follow I provide a variety of liturgical elements that highlight the affirmation of the body through dance. I also provide a sermon about dance in scripture that affirms the body.

Liturgical Elements about Dance
Prayer of Invocation:

> Dancing God, move among us and within us, we pray. Teach us your steps that we may move toward wholeness and peace. As we dance with you and with our community of faith, move us toward spaces where we can create peace and stand for justice. May our dances embody your transformational love and compassion as we worship you now and always. Amen.

Call to Worship (Psalm 150)

> Leader: Praise the Lord!
> Community: Praise God in the sanctuary!
> Leader: Praise God for mighty deeds, according to God's greatness!
> Community: Praise God with trumpet and harp!
> Leader: Praise God with drums and dancing!
> Community: Praise God with strings and pipes!
> Leader: Praise God with clanging cymbals!

All: Let everything that has breath praise the Lord!

Doxology (multiple tunes)

This is a doxology I wrote that can be used to multiple hymn tunes. If you add "hallelujah, hallelujah" after the second line and "hallelujah, hallelujah, hallelujah, hallelujah, hallelujah" after the last line, it also works to the tune LASST UNS ERFREUEN.

Praise God the Painter of the Sky
Praise Christ inspiring Songs on High
Praise Spirit Dancing Wild and Free
Praise all Creative Unity.

Embodied Ritual: Redeeming the Body

The ritual of Redeeming the Body involves providing a safe space for persons to reclaim the primacy of their bodies and redeem them with words and acts of affirmation and wholeness. I typically include calming music—drumming, instrumental, or ocean sounds—in the background and invite the people gathered to close their eyes. With eyes closed, they are invited to focus all of their attention on their hands. They are invited to imagine that they hold within their hands all of the judgment and shame that has been heaped upon their body. This judgment and shame may have come from the church or popular culture or both.

Acknowledging how this shame and judgment runs deep within our gendered bodies, people are invited to mold their hands into a shape or gesture that embodies that shame, pain, fear, and judgment. This shape may be ugly or even painful to hold. Gnarled knuckles or clenched fists are sometimes the best way to hold this shame. After the shape is formed with the hands, people are invited to wash their hands down over their body to their feet. Naming in their minds and hearts the shame and judgment that has been heaped upon their feet, they are invited to wash their gnarled hands or clenched fists—or whatever shape their hands have taken—over their feet. They are then invited to wash their hands up over their legs and repeat the same thoughts and gestures, naming in their minds the shame and judgment that has been heaped upon their legs. This same routine continues as hands wash over the hips, stomach, chest, back, shoulders, arms, and head, each time inviting participants to recall the hurt and shame those body parts have experienced. Once the leader finishes guiding the group through every body part, participants are invited to release their hands, as though they are letting go of all the judgment and shame they have been holding. For some, this action of release is physically freeing because they have gnarled their hands or clenched their fists so tightly. For others, the action is emotionally and spiritually freeing, as well.

Then the ritual repeats itself with different intentions. Focusing once again on the hands, they are invited to fill their hands with grace, acceptance, affirmation, and love, molding their hands into a gesture or shape that holds these positive emotions. The hands and fingers typically relax and often people open their hands as though they are about to receive a gift. After the shape is formed with the hands, people are invited to wash their hands down over their body to their feet. Naming in their minds and hearts the fact that their feet are beloved, worthy, and honored. The person leading the ritual could proclaim that their feet are made in the image of God, or that they guide us to way of peace, or some other scriptural admonition about feet. Then the entire process repeats, moving up the body and pausing with words of redemption and affirmation at each body part: legs, hips, stomach, chest, back, shoulders, arms, and head. After concluding with the head, participants are invited to open their eyes and see their bodies anew, redeemed, and affirmed.

While the ritual may seem repetitive on paper or simple in nature, I have experienced it on many occasions being incredibly empowering and redeeming for those participating. Witnessing someone wipe away tears of celebration or leave the ritual holding their heads a little higher, their chest more lifted as they walk out of the space with their body affirmed and redeemed is no small thing. The redemption of the body is no small thing.

Sermon for the Affirmed Body
Misunderstood Scriptures, Misunderstood Dancers
2 Samuel 6 and Mark 6

Like many churches all over the world, our church follows the Revised Common Lectionary. This is a rotation of scriptures that provides a text from the Hebrew bible, Psalms, Gospels, and Epistles each Sunday of the year in a cycle of three years. Each quarter, I look through the lections and determine preaching themes for the season. There are days when I celebrate with a nerdy hurrah because I like the texts listed and there are days when I stare that texts and wonder what on earth I'm going to say.

And then there are the rare jewels, when the Revised Common Lectionary selects texts so wonderful, so perfect, so interesting that I can barely contain myself. Today, my friends, is one of those days. I imagine that most preachers spent their week sloughing through commentaries while trying to determine how to preach about David's revealing dance and Salome's dance that seemed to lead to the beheading of John the Baptist. As you know, however, I'm not "most preachers." Rather, I am a former professional dancer who has dedicated all of my research and writing to the intersections between dance and religion.

So, when I read the texts from 2 Samuel and Mark 6, it's as though the heavens opened and I saw the angels dancing. Only one other time in the three year cycle of scriptures do we get texts about dance and that's when we read about Miriam dancing on the shores of freedom after crossing the sea of Reeds with her little brother, Moses, in Exodus. There are many, many others, mind you, but the lectionary only gives us these few.

So, let's dig in! First, we have this rich text from 2 Samuel about the role of the body in ritual events, about the need for dance in worship. King David is joined by 30,000 others in bringing the Ark of the Covenant from the House of Obed-Edom. We can probably agree that it's likely that there weren't exactly 30,000 people, but that is no matter. The point is that there were *a lot* of people and that their worship was celebration at its finest. Mind you, worship can be reverent. Worship can express lament. Worship can embody transcendence. But in 2 Samuel, David and the other Israelites were so caught in the grips of God's joy that their worship is best described as celebration.

They had songs. They had lyres. They had harps and tambourines and drums and castanets and cymbals. It was a raucous time. In the midst of it all—between God's glory shining forth from the ark and the pulse of the music—David got caught up in the spirit. 2 Samuel tells us that "David danced before the Lord with all his might."

Shouting people. Clanging symbols. Beating drums. Pulsating music. Dionysian abandon. Ecstatic worship. A dancing king. All the words are active. It's as though the Hebrew language in the passage thrusts us forward, our bodies responding with kinesthetic identification, as we, too become caught up in the celebration. And then the text pauses with an interesting tidbit of information that is not the slightest bit related to movement or worship or celebration.

It is a precarious description of this dancing king. "David was girded with a linen ephod." We are left scratching our heads, wondering what this odd descriptive detail has to do with King David's worship. And then the action continues. Dancing David, the musicians, the shouting people, and the ark came into the city of David and "Michal, daughter of Saul looked out of the window, and saw King David leaping and dancing before the LORD; and she despised him in her heart."

This is where many preachers and scholars jump to swift conclusions and demonize David's wife, Michal, quickly elevating David as God's ultimate rock star and claiming that Michal was too pagan or too prudish or lacked the spirit. Such scholars pay no mind that David was essentially "revealing his glory" to the whole city as he writhes and whirls in his linen ephod. Lest you need to look up ephod on your smart phone, it is pretty much a loin cloth. Interestingly, wearing such a revealing garment was prohibited in worship precisely because bowing, prostrating, and dancing were such essential parts of ancient Israelite worship.

So, I would like to propose two theories for why Michal despised David when he danced before the Lord with all his might. If we read the entire book of 1 Samuel and the beginning of 2 Samuel we'll notice that David had a deep and abiding love for someone else before he married Michal. Like the good soap opera that the bible is, David's previous lover was none other than Michal's brother, Jonathan. Now, this is another topic for another sermon, but scripture is quite clear that David loved Jonathan more than any other woman. They kissed and shared garments and David was broken when Jonathan died…so broken that he agreed to a political marriage with Jonathan's sister Michal. A lot of heteronormative commentators gloss over this, claiming that David and Jonathan were the epitome of best friends, but if you really translate the Hebrew it's clear that they were lovers. And yet David marries Michal and she despises him. You might also despise someone if you had to marry them when you knew they were actually in love with your dead brother.

A second theory comes from understanding the vital nuances of dance history. Namely, that all dancing in worship for ancient Israelites was communal. Rarely did someone perform a solo dance, but instead all the Israelites would gather together, hand-in-hand to worship Yahweh with heart, mind, soul, *and* body. David, therefore, was abusing his power as king by stepping into the worship realm, clad in a forbidden cloth, and dancing about like a soloist. So, rather than demonizing Michal as one who lacked the spirit and wouldn't worship fully like David did, it's important to remember that David was not only revealing "his glory" to anyone who caught a glimpse of his spirit-bound leaps, but he was also leaving others out by making a show of his dance rather than dancing hand-in-hand with his worshiping community.

Before we say more about that, let's make the several thousand years leap to the Gospel of Mark to examine the dance of Salome. If you were listening carefully to the text from Mark, you're probably wondering why I'm talking about someone named Salome. There was no mention of anyone named Salome in the text. Rather, in the Markan text both the dancing daughter and her mother are named Herodias. In Matthew's text, the daughter is nameless. It wasn't until later when Josephus, a Jewish historian, named her Salome, though he never claimed that she was guilty for the beheading of the John the Baptist.

Since Josephus made up this name, interpreters have gone crazy with blame, ruining the poor little girl's reputation. The more prominent John became in history, the more infamous Salome became. This is reflected in art, as well. In 1462 we have Gozzoli's rendering of Salome, which shows the dance of an innocent child doing gymnastics and twirling the way many little children do when given the spotlight. Perhaps Gozzoli translated Greek in addition to producing famous paintings, because it's clear that the word used to described "Salome" is *thugatar* which means "little daughter." Based solely on what the text says, and even these early artistic renderings, it's obvious that this scripture is about a little girl dancing for play and fun and then being taken advantage of by a conniving mother and uncle.

We wonder, then, why Salome gets such a bad rap. I've heard many avid church goers point to Salome when describing why they don't want dance in worship. It's as though dance is the next step on the slippery slope toward beheading prophets. You see, with the development of the femme fatale in 19th and 20th century art, film, and literature, Salome's story was quickly exaggerated. Gustave Moreau painted over one hundred images of Salome in the 1870s, all illustrating a seductive woman in gauzy fabric. Then Oscar Wilde wrote his infamous play, *Salome*, and it is clear that he never bothered to even read the accounts from the Gospels because his play includes an adult Salome flirting with John the Baptist, stripping down to a dance of seven veils, and then kissing the severed head on a bloody platter in 1894.

Then performing artists went wild (pun intended) with the story. Richard Strauss composed an opera, Loie Fuller and Maude Allan choreographed dances that are little more than a strip tease as they embody the "dance of seven veils." Amidst it all, a little girl's reputation is destroyed and dance is demonized as nothing more than an agent of seduction and slander. In these ways, popular culture impacts our understanding of Salome's dance even more than the bible does!

If we chalk the plays, the opera, the paintings, and the choreography up to extreme poetic licensing, then perhaps we can return to the heart of the text. And we'll see the story of a little girl who was asked to dance by a family member at a party. I have many such memories from my own childhood as I cried "Watch me! Watch me!" to parents, aunts, uncles, and grandparents while I leapt and twirled, filled with the child-like innocence that we adults often forget when it comes to worship. I am convinced that Salome's dance was no different.

In fact, I think that both of our texts for this morning teach us two similar lessons. The first is that many stories in scripture are difficult to understand. David's dance is most often glorified as one who intimately knows the heart of God. Salome's dance is most often vilified as a twisted erotic dance of desire. But, as we have seen, neither of these interpretations clings to the heart of these scriptures. Rather, our readings of the text have been colored by culture, art, and the bias of patriarchal commentators over the centuries. One can only wonder if the stories would be received differently if the genders were reversed. What if Michal danced and revealed her glory and David despised her? What if little boy Herod danced before Queen Salome? Would artists, commentators, and culture have interpreted their tales differently?

We can only wonder. So, these fascinating texts teach us that much lies beneath the surface of scripture. Hidden in the crevices of the text, embedded in the very language of the bible, are nuances that often go overlooked if we do not pay enough attention.

More important than this, is that both texts harken us back to our primal bodily roots of worship. Both David and Salome remind us of the power of the body in worshipping a God who cannot be confined by words, limited by language, or illustrated by image. Texts like these make us recall that our ancestors worshiped God with music, spoken word, and dance, their bodies, hearts, minds, and voices uniting in a way that was pleasing to God. When we check our bodies at the door and leave worship only to our minds, hearts, and voices, then we are forsaking our history.

The dances of David and Salome remind us that there are times when we become so caught up in the unbridled ecstasy of God's life-changing love that our bodies simply must respond.

There are moments when you draw so near to the heart of God that your body cannot contain the joy. This is why, in the New Testament, the Greek word for exceedingly joyful, *aggallio* literally means "with very much leaping," or to put it in contemporary terms, "to jump for joy."

It's important to worship God with your mind. That's why we translate and read historical contexts and exegete. Because the mind is a vital part of our worship. It's important to worship God with your heart. That's why we share personal experiences of why our faith is so meaningful. Because the heart is a vital part of our worship. It's important to worship God with our voices. That's why we sing and pray aloud. Because the voice is a vital part of worship.

But it's also important to worship God with your body. We are the *body* of Christ, after all. Living, breathing, moving, dancing. Just like David and Salome. Just like Miriam and Jephthah's daughter and the Shulamite and Judith and even Jesus. Because our bodies are holy. Our bodies are redeemed. And when we dance, our bodies worship. It doesn't get much holier than that. Amen.

Conclusions: When the Body is Affirmed

Preaching and worship looks, feels, and sounds differently when the body is affirmed, honored, and celebrated through dance. Whether it is the embodied Hallelujahs of a group of Baptists who dance on Easter Sunday, the myriad dances hidden in the crevices of the sacred cannon, the church dancing in worship throughout thousands of years of history, or the theological concepts of Trinity, creation, incarnation, and community, bodies are affirmed through the act of dancing. And these affirmed and gendered bodies change our preaching and worship. They remind us that the Word can be proclaimed, not merely in spoken word, but with the body. And when the body preaches on our behalf, it is very holy, indeed.

Chapter 7

The Body Gone Awry: Preaching, Worship, and Disordered Eating

SINCE AS MANY AS TEN MILLION AMERICAN FEMALES struggle with Anorexia Nervosa or Bulimia Nervosa, it is evident that the disordered body must be addressed in preaching and worship.[126] The matter becomes even more poignant when we recognize that clinicians estimate that eighty to eighty-five percent of women have a Sub-clinical Eating Disorder (SED). SED describes individuals who are obsessed with weight and body image and is characterized by chronic under-eating, over-exercising, and binge-eating resulting from long periods of self-starvation. What is more, in the United States, the statistics for women of color, of ethnic and racial minorities, and of poor women are now nearly the same as white women from privileged backgrounds. The way culture portrays and values emaciated bodies now impacts the bodies of women across racial and socio-economic lines in ways never before seen. These women surely sit in our pews, worship in our communities, and even preach behind our pulpits. Preachers and worshippers are not immune to such disorders. In fact, the abuse of theology and scripture often contribute to the body gone awry.

---

[126] All statistics and descriptions of eating disorders are from "Eating Disorders." *Diagnostic and Statistical Manual of Mental Disorder – IV—TR*, 4th ed. (Washington, D.C.: American Psychiatric Association, 2000), 583-95. Interestingly, recent statistical research indicates that eating disorders are growing among racial and ethnic minorities in the United States. In these ways, the old adage that anorexia or bulimia is a disordered of the upper-middle class white girl no longer rings true.

In determining how to more fully incorporate the body—and all of its pains—into preaching and worship, I examine scripture, history, theology, and theories in preaching and worship. My starting point, however, is personal experience. While eating disorders plagued much of my adolescence and early adulthood, I begin with my observations as a young seminarian grappling with the role my religion in the self-imposed starvation that riddled so much of my life. After a personal story and an examination of scripture, history, and theology, I provide two practical ways for preachers to address disordered eating in preaching and worship.

Starving for Salvation

Beginning in seminary, I was in what I thought was the recovery period of a long battle with eating disorders. Though I struggled to name and receive proper treatment for it due to my poor background, anorexia plagued much of my middle and high school years and I suffered from bulimia for my first two years of college. Amidst the transition from college to graduate school, a new ministry, new relationships, and beginning to feel comfortable with myself as a feminist, I began classes in seminary and a new staff position at a local church, proudly breaking one hundred pound mark at age twenty-two.

During the initial phase of this transition, however, my disorder emerged in a new form of bulimia: compulsive-over-exercising. I ran eight to ten miles a day, six days a week in addition to weight training and other cardio. Since my body was oppressed by my neglect and abuse, I had not yet transitioned from a child's body to a woman's, even in my twenties. After I quit running adamantly, however, my body responded to no longer being a college "athlete" (I was a college cheerleader for four years) by gaining fifteen pounds. What felt like suddenly, my clothes no longer fit and I "filled out," as an older male minister once noted. With this, I was not comfortable. In addition to physical changes, I was grappling with Obsessive Compulsive Behaviors and a tremendous guilt complex that I was not good enough (i.e.: skinny enough).

As an artist, I attempted to paint and dance my anxiety and fears, noticing, however, the difference in my body as I moved. Also as an artist, I studied art as I sought to learn more about the role of art and religion. Popular or "traditional" depictions of Jesus had always been troubling for me. I had long struggled with portrayals, such as Warner Sallman's 1940 Euro Jesus, that white-washed Jesus, painting him with fair skin, blue eyes, and blond hair; I found the Westernized Jesus inaccurate and oppressive for many other cultures. Furthermore, I had struggled with depictions of the crucifixion for some time, as it appears to be a glorification of violence and pain, aspects to which I felt the church dedicates far too much time. If we, indeed, worship the "prince" of peace rather than the god of bloody, sacrificed, violence, then why do these scenes hang all over the walls of our churches? At this juncture, however, it was not the color of Jesus' skin or hair, or the gruesome, bloody violence that haunted my thoughts. Rather, it was the emaciated depiction of Jesus' body.

As a young woman, seeking to recover from years of eating disorders, I stared at crucified depictions of my savior, such as Mathias Grunewald's: the embodiment of love, compassion, and service, the One toward which I should strive to be, the One I should imitate. On that cross I saw my model of perfection: beaten, bloody, with protruding hip bones, able to count his bony rib cage, an empty stomach yet showing a defined and sculpted abdomen, thin yet muscular arms, and cheeks sunken into a face withered with hunger. As I looked at the One I am called to imitate, I realized that, at the nadir of my disorder, if someone had stripped me bare, spread my arms out in the shape of a cross, and painted a picture of me, I would have, indeed, imitated this crucified Jesus. We were identical, at least our bodies were. Despite the fact that Jesus was distinctly male,[127] the properly placed loin cloth would render us twins if our hypothetical paintings were hung side-by-side, for my body had wasted away with no fat to portray any femininity as breasts;

---

[127] Although some feminist theologians find the maleness of Jesus problematic, I recognize that the incarnation occurred during a time of intense patriarchy. I agree with Russell's proposition that the maleness of Jesus is incidental, whereas the humanity of Jesus is paramount. This concept is discussed further in the theological section of this chapter.

our hips both rubbed sores on our skin, our ribs could be counted, and our suffering was portrayed through the emaciation of our depleted bodies. Jesus' blood was from thorns, nails, and a spear. Mine was from an acid-worn esophagus, coughing up blood into the comfort of a dorm-room toilet.

As a "filled-out" young seminarian, I gazed at these depictions of my God, I remembered how I used to look, and I found myself in the grip of an odd logic. Is this what it means to imitate Jesus? Shall I, again, "take up my cross" and follow Christ? Is this the load I need to bear? Rationale and logic screams, "Of course not! We are called to imitate Christ's actions of love and justice, liberation and hope. It does not mean that you have look like Jesus or suffer like Jesus!" Or does it?

Throughout history, art and icons seem tell us otherwise. They send mixed and oppressive messages to the disordered eater. Shall we allow these visual messages, powerful messages, to hang in our churches as portrayals of that toward which we strive? Shall we allow depictions of glorified violence and utter starvation to influence members of our churches, possibly struggling with eating disorders, and certainly influenced by the contradictory glorification and abuse of the body in American culture?

I know that Jesus fasted and suffered. Perhaps some depictions, though likely not popularized ones, are relatively accurate. I am not denying the suffering of Christ. I find my struggle in our obsession with Jesus' emaciated body. Are we not crucifying the anorexic and bulimic along with Jesus when we display these pictures in our sanctuaries? Are these visual representations merely hammering the nails into the hands of suffering women and men that struggle enough with body image and confidence? Furthermore, is the theology we espouse from many of our pulpits and hymnals, that proclaims a substitutionary atonement where it "should be me on the cross," furthering the sense of guilt, inadequacy, and hurt that struggling anorexics see when they gaze at their crucified Lord? Is this what we are called to look like? Who is hanging on the cross today?

Scripture and the Crucified Anorexic

Unfortunately, in the search for finding a visual depiction of the crucifixion that provides liberation for the disordered eater, biblical scholarship is ostensibly silent. The scriptures are mute in describing the way Christ's body looked on the cross, or on the way a healthy body must look. The bible does shed light on various issues that apply to the role of eating disorders in the preaching and worship.

Ephesians admonishes believers to "be imitators of God, as beloved children, and live in love, as Christ loved us and gave himself up for us, a fragrant offering and sacrifice to God (Ephesians 5:1-2 NRSV)." Preaching from such a text seems like a powerful way to call worshippers to be more loving and kind, as one may rationally deduce that living in love is an imitation of God. Yet, for the disordered eater, typically struggling with extreme perfectionism, imitating Christ entails replicating to perfection. The craving for perfection is a recurring idiom in anorexic and bulimic discourse. Psychology traces an anorexic woman's perfectionism to a host of underlying distorted concepts, especially an enigmatic low self esteem.[128] The suffering, the emaciation, the picture of a hungry body is the apex of emulation. As the emaciated Christ's rib cage protrudes through his chest in many artistic renderings of the crucifixion, an anorexic woman describes the imitation of perfection toward which she strives as she states, "I stood sideways, naked in the mirror, and realized that I literally had almost no flesh left. Where my rear used to be was a pointed bone. All of my ribs stuck out; I thought it was perfectly beautiful."[129] Moreover, the notion of Jesus' suffering also provides opportunities for imitation as another disordered eater describes life:

> The whole life is like you are carrying a cross—something heroic, something that is very difficult and demands admiration. I felt [that] doing something

[128] Michelle Mary Lelwica, *Starving for Salvation* (New York: Oxford University Press, 1999), 106-113.
[129] Lelwica., 113.

> that was not hard was quite inconceivable; it would be lazy and despicable. [130]

Portions of the passion narrative also provide a myriad of ways in which scripture influences artistic interpretations of Jesus' body on the cross. John 19:28 records Jesus as saying, "I am thirsty." As the anorexic's cries of hunger reveal suffering and helplessness, so too, do Jesus' words on the cross. In addition, Jesus cries out on the cross, "Father, forgive them; they do not know what they are doing (Luke 23:34)." It is not the plea of forgiveness on behalf of another that could be troubling for the disordered eater, but the patriarchal undertones associated with Jesus' reference to God as father. Margo Maine dedicates an entire book to the study of father-daughter relationships for women with disordered eating. She notes that many anorexic and bulimic women suffer from "father hunger." "Father hunger is a deep, persistent desire for emotional connection with the father . . . [it] refers to this unfulfilled longing for father, which for girls and women, often translates into conflicts about food and weight."[131] A young woman describes this feeling when she states, "my dad would often focus on my fatness and slowness, telling me not to be lazy . . . both when I was starving myself, and when my father hit me, I wished to be as small as possible."[132]

Is father-language healthy for this woman? Many feminist theologians suggest that speaking of God gynomorphically (Mother or Goddess) rather than anthropomorphically (Father) would acknowledge that father-language represents the "necrophilia of patriarchy," and substituting mother-language could provide liberation.[133] Therefore, it is evident that, even before a preacher begins to pen her sermon, the very language surrounding the passion event and the role of Christ-like imitation can prove problematic for the disordered eater. It is our responsibility, as preachers and leaders

---

[130] Lelwica, 109.

[131] Margo Maine, *Father Hunger: Fathers, Daughters and Food* (Carlsbad: Gurse Books, 1991), 3.

[132] Lelwica, 63.

[133] Grant, 164.

of worship, to acknowledge these complexities and to try and read scripture through the lens of a disordered eater. In the same way that feminists urge homeleticians to approach the text with a hermeneutic of suspicion, preachers must engage the text by asking what it teaches us about the abused body.

Church History and the Crucified Anorexic

Glimpses of these emaciated images of crucifixion in art history and the historical evidence of eating disorders associated with mystic women illuminate ways in which the contemporary preacher may approach disordered eating from the pulpit and in worship. The art serves as a visual history, a visual text that illustrates how Christians portrayed the body. And the fasting, starvation, and self-induced vomiting of mystic women remind us that today's woman is not alone in her struggle with food and body image.

Robin Jensen's work regarding the suffering and dead Christ in early Christian art is of paramount importance when attempting to understand the development of the church's obsession with depicting the crucifixion through art.[134] She notes that early church images never show Jesus suffering, dying, or resurrected. Debatably, the oldest known artistic depiction of Christ crucified is dated around 430 C.E. Jensen notes that "a demonstrated incompatibility between artistic creations and theological writings has been taken to indicate that art serves in some sense as a corrective mechanism."[135]

By the tenth century, E.J. Tinsley proposes that Christ is not depicted on the cross because onlookers may become confused and believe that Jesus is still dead, rather than resurrected.[136] As in the Middle Ages, where the crucifix was a dominant feature of church organization and a token of suffering

---

[134] The remainder of information regarding depictions of the crucifixion from the beginning of the early church through the fourth century all comes from Robin Jensen, "The Suffering and Dead Christ in Early Christian Art," *ARTS* (August 2001): 22-28.

[135] Jensen.

[136] E.J. Tinsely, "The Coming of a Dead and Naked Christ," *Religion* 2 (1972): 24-36.

and death,[137] images in the Renaissance provided theological meaning predominantly for illiterate people until at least the sixteenth century.[138] Therefore, education occurred by recognizing the premeditated theological significance of the artistic renderings. Not only were the majority of the depictions of the crucifix emaciated, they also appeared nude with an emphasis on the genitalia of Christ.[139] Steinberg claims that Renaissance art was the first and last phase of Christian art to claim full Christian orthodoxy in the acknowledgment of the entirety of incarnation, "the upper and lower body together, not excluding even the body's sexual component."[140] In regard to the disordered female eater, it is important to note that the nude Christ served the "Renaissance man visual images that confirmed his precariously inflated self-image . . . Moreover the appearance of God in the male sex was understood as privileging that sex. Explicit visual depictions of Christ's male genitals reinforced the identifications of men with Christ."[141] The Renaissance produced art at the hands of men depicting men. Joan Kelly-Gadol asks if women even had a Renaissance.[142]

In addition to the role of Jesus' emaciated male body in art history, the role of disordered eating in female mystics is also worth consideration. Long before slenderness was the hallmark of the ideal female body, fasting was a way for women to define themselves. "The refusal or inability to eat, and sometimes the need to vomit, played a central role in late medieval women's piety. From about 1200 to 1500 C.E., these practices were a means for cultivating the religious ideal of suffering with Christ."[143] It appears that fasting practices were much more

---

[137] Regnerus Steensma, "The Image of Christ in Contemporary British Art," *ARTS* (December 2001): 31

[138] Margaret Miles, "Nudity, Gender, and Religious Meaning in the Italian Renaissance," in *Art as Religious Studies*, ed. Doug Adams and Diane Apostolos-Cappodona (New York: Crossroads Publishing, 1987), 103.

[139] Miles, 104.

[140] Miles, 104.

[141] Miles, 111.

[142] Miles, 110.

[143] Lelwica, 27.

extreme among the female monastics. Jerome believed that female asceticism was for the purpose of renouncing "the 'natural' female function of sexuality and procreation."[144] Historical authors refer to this as anorexia mirabilis, or the miraculous loss of appetite.[145] "Whether anorexia is holy [mirabilis] or nervous [nervosa] depends on the culture in which a young woman strives to gain control in her life."[146]

For the female monastic, fasting became a way to conquer the feminine-looking nature of her body. Her body withers and becomes "masculine" in nature, her breasts become dry, her voice becomes scratchy, her menstruation ceases, she begins to grow fur to warm her emaciated skin, and her sexual danger to men lessens. Even mystics greatly admired, such as Catherine of Sienna, struggled with disordered eating. She reportedly lived on the Eucharist alone, gave away her food to the hungry, and stuck twigs down her throat to induce vomiting.[147] "For medieval women, hunger, food, fasting, and feeding were *the* central means and metaphors for becoming one with Christ's suffering, for achieving holiness, and for saving souls."[148] It is not difficult to imagine a female monastic gazing at the crucifix worn around her neck as she denies herself the intake of any nourishment besides Eucharist.

Most religious feminists would agree that "the antiwoman bias of the Judeo-Christian tradition has played a defining role in instructing women that our bodies are flawed and in need of correction."[149] Men in power—priests and theologians—told these women that their bodies were objects of shame. Other men in power—artists and sculptors—followed suit by showing these women what their bodies should be like: the emaciated and suffering Christ. It is the responsibility of the preacher to use words and images to begin the process of healing for women throughout the history of the church who have been

---

[144] Teresa Shaw, *The Burden of the Flesh: Fasting and Sexuality in Early Christianity* (Minneapolis: Fortress Press, 1998), 239.
[145] Lelwica, 27.
[146] Lelwica, 27.
[147] Lelwica, 27.
[148] Lelwica, 27.
[149] Lelwica, 44.

shamed from the pulpit, their bodies degraded by patriarchal preachers. The time has come for women's bodies to be praised, embraced, included, and reminded that they are created in the image of God and nothing less. The first step just may be for that struggling female body to step into the pulpit and preach.

Theology and the Crucified Anorexic

Foremost in addressing theological issues are the particularity of the incarnation and contextual theories of atonement. What theology are these emaciated images of Christ espousing for the disordered eater? Do these crucified images represent a theology of liberation and wholeness or depravity and shame? In addressing the particularity of the incarnation, Jacquelyn Grant clearly states, "It is my claim that there is a direct relationship between our perception of Jesus Christ and our perception of ourselves."[150] For this reason, the doctrine of Christology, from its initial formulated inception, has been problematic for women. Not only does the anorexic female need to heal her image of an emaciated Christ, but the particularity of Jesus' sex can prove problematic, as well.

In light of this discussion two questions are critical: Can women redeem Jesus? And can Jesus redeem women? Rita Nakashima Brock addresses these questions simultaneously: "The doctrine that only a male form can incarnate God fully and be salvific makes our individual lives in female bodies a prison against God and denies our actual, sensual, changing selves as the lover of divine activity."[151] Not only does the anorexic female need to heal her image of an emaciated Christ, but the particularity of Jesus' sex can prove problematic, as well.

In addition, contextual atonement is critical. Often historical theories, like Anselm's satisfaction theory of atonement or Abelard's moral theory, are not entirely applicable to contemporary contexts and cultures. Rather, contextual theories of atonement are needed. Most pertinent to such contextualized theologies are representations of a crucified woman. Janet Walton speaks of the double scandal of the cross

---

[150] Grant, 63.
[151] Brock, 68.

in New York, 1984. The Cathedral of St. John the Divine took the daring step of portraying Edwina Sandy's sculpture *Christa*, which depicted a woman hanging on the cross.[152] The same year, Union Theological Seminary utilized a small clay figure, *Christine on the Cross*, in the chapel during Holy Week. The sculptor, James Murphy, turned the cross upside down and carved a statue of a woman standing with both her arms nailed to the vertical section of the cross, with her legs spread on the lower cross bar, "expressing the violence and hostility of both physical and emotional rape."[153] Walton notes:

> Both crucifixes challenged the literal historical interpretation of the cross. They expressed an evolving interpretation which sees all humanity participating in the pain of crucifixion. In "Christine on the Cross" a statement of hostility and humiliation heaped upon women in the form of rape and submission is visibly portrayed . . . The sculpture identified these women and women of all ages as suffering servants who have been wounded, broken and forsaken because of our inequities.[154]

When we acknowledge the importance of contextual Christology, we must address that, in some contexts, "the cross put no final end to the reign of evil, for there crucifixion recurs all over again . . . We cannot give our victims the cross, for they are already its true bearers . . . In the world of victims, our language of victory—the language of redemption—may alienate, echoing only the speech of oppressors."[155] In order to be theologically responsible, we must acknowledge the theology espoused by our images of Christ and ask ourselves, "who hangs on the cross today?" Christ has risen. The anorexic, however, remains crucified. Were you there when they crucified my Lord?

---

[152] Janet Walton, *Worship and the Arts: A Vital Connection* (Collegeville: The Liturgical Press, 1988), 105.
[153] Walton, 106.
[154] Walton, 106.
[155] Plank, 965-66.

Preaching, Worship, and the Crucified Anorexic

Scripture, history, and theology combine with the theoretical side of preaching and liturgy so that we can eventually reach their practical side. Primary in preaching about eating disorders is the use of testimony in the work of Anna Carter Florence.[156] Primary in developing liturgy that acknowledges eating disorders is Andrea Bieler's concept of sacramental permeability.[157]

Florence's work on testimony is beautifully recounted in her book, *Preaching as Testimony*, where she adheres to the classical definition of testimony. She defines testimony as both a narration of events and a confession about what we believe about those events. "A sermon in the testimony tradition," she writes, "is not an autobiography but a very particular kind of proclamation: the preacher tells what she has seen and heard *in the biblical text and in life*, and then confesses what she believes about it."[158] Such preaching offers women (and men) the opportunity to proclaim the truth of their experiences with eating disorders in relation to the biblical text. When preaching about fasting, Lent, Jesus' time in the wilderness, communion, or manna falling from heaven, the disordered eater's life experiences testify to some of the unspoken nuances of the biblical text. Their testimonies, then, can be incredibly powerful when proclaimed from the pulpit. What is more, their testimony, their preaching, also gives agency and voice to the countless others within the congregation who have experienced similar struggles. Florence elaborates further:

> For every time a woman stood up to proclaim the gospel, her community saw, in its very reaction to her, a reflection of itself: what is believed, what structures ordered its life together, what views it held about power and privilege, who was and was not allowed to speak truth. In standing up to preach,

---

[156] Anna Carter Florence, *Preaching as Testimony* (Louisville: Westminster John Knox, 2007).

[157] Andrea Bieler and Luise Schottroff, *The Eucharist: Bodies, Bread, and Resurrection* (Minneapolis: Fortress Press, 2007).

[158] Florence, xii.

> these women stood in their own lives in such a way that the community could see the truth about itself, laid bare and exposed in the light of God's Word. Women embodied for their listeners the announcement that the Word became flesh and dwells among us—even the flesh of women's [broken] bodies.[159]

Here, Florence is speaking specifically to the power and efficacy of the testimonial preaching of Anne Hutchinson, Sarah Osborn, and Jarena Lee, three women who preached and testified when women were otherwise excluded from the pulpit. But her words ring true when it comes to the proclamation of the disordered eater. Can the Word become flesh in the broken and suffering body of a disordered eater? The preaching and testimony of disordered eaters from the pulpit would answer "yes!" The Word becomes flesh in aching, suffering, starving bodies. These bodies are also a part of the body of Christ.

What is more, preaching as testimony not only provides avenues for women to name and proclaim their disorder, it also provides the opportunity for them to work toward healing. Florence contends that "preaching is not just proclaiming good news; it is *making* good news, right here and now."[160] In this way, stepping into the pulpit and proclaiming a testimony of disordered eating can become a redemptive act. The power of naming it aloud brings healing. Testifying one's suffering when you proclaim the good news of the Co-Sufferer is redemptive and healing. The preaching of the disordered eater not only brings healing to the one proclaiming, but also to listeners. I recall, for example, preaching about eating disorders in relation to communion. When I uttered the phrase, "Do you know how many calories are in the body of Christ, broken for you? The disordered eater probably does," I noticed a quiet woman in the back pew begin to cry. Following worship she approached me with tears of gratitude, claiming that she never imagined that anyone else in the entire world struggled with communion in that way. Voicing my own struggle, preaching as testimony, helped

---

[159] Florence, 57.
[160] Florence, 107.

this quiet woman take the first steps toward healing her own disorder. This story of communion leads to Andrea Bieler's liturgical work on sacramental permeability.

The notion of sacramental permeability takes seriously the realities of human bodies as a central part of communion. Bieler contends that "sacramental worship embraces a permeability in which the bread we consume at our kitchen tables, the bread we steal from the poor, and the bread that is consecrated and consumed during Holy Communion are related."[161] When we approach communion through the lens of Bieler's sacramental permeability, we realize that the bread that is denied to the poor is the same bread upon which we feast. The wine that tempts the alcoholic is the same wine imbibed in remembrance. The bread that the bulimic purges is the same bread that we say unites all Christians. The bread and cup that we call holy are the same bread and cup that many call addiction, temptation, disorder, allergy, or desire. What does communion mean for them? What does the sacrament of communion mean for the disordered eater?

Understanding the lived reality of sacramental permeability is best described in a personal story. The story occurred after I first began attending church as a teenager. A friend from school whom I'd been helping get his grades and life together decided to attend with me when the youth group was having a communion service. His name was Big Scotty. Our youth minister explained that, on this evening, our communion would focus on our community. So, rather than taking the bread and the cup for ourselves, we could tear a piece, dip it in the cup and offer it to another in the youth group, as way of sharing, saying thank you for friendship, or reconciling with one another. I sat silently in my seat, praying that no one would offer me communion. The loaf was big and sourdough and the juice was filled with sugar. I glared at those elements with contempt. Do you know how many calories are in the body of Christ, broken for you? I did. And I could not fathom eating them. As a 17 year-old anorexic, the thought of chewing and swallowing what appeared to be about 130 calories made me sick to my stomach.

---

[161] Bieler, 5.

My prayers were not answered. Instead Big Scotty approached me, communion elements in hand, and said, "You've helped me so much, that I tore a big hunk of Jesus for you," as he handed me a massive chunk of bread dripping with sweet and sugary grape juice.

"What am I supposed to do?" I thought. "If I don't accept it, I'll look like a jerk, but if I eat it I'll get fat." So, I ate the 130 calories worth of communion and began to cry, sob, actually. Everyone thought I was moved by the service of communion, by Big Scotty's heart-felt gesture, and that made me feel even worse. I wasn't moved by the sacrifice of Christ or by Scotty's gratitude, I was crying because I knew how much fat I'd just eaten. What a horrible person I was for worrying about issues as pedestrian, shallow, and privileged as calories in such a holy and sacred space. I excused myself. Everyone thought I was going get tissues to wipe away my tears of devotion, but I was actually going to purge. The body of Christ filled the youth room toilet. Disordered eating is a communion issue; it is a liturgical issue.

Beiler's concept of sacramental permeability gives worship leaders the tools and methods for approaching such complex issues. Acknowledging in liturgy that the bread we break is the body of Christ *and* the calories shunned by the anorexic is powerful. Acknowledging in liturgy that we are the body of Christ and the body of Christ is made up of all kinds of bodies—aching, aging, growing, suffering, desiring, broken and even disordered—is powerful. In these ways, voicing the struggles of the disordered eater within the context of worship does not feel "other," profane, or unrelated, but through the lens of sacramental permeability it is a vital part of the communion event, a vital part of liturgy.

The hymns we sing, the liturgies we read, the Word we proclaim holds power over the disordered eater. Hymns, liturgies, and sermons that emphasize total depravity, shame, or the patriarchal particularity of Jesus' maleness have the power to wreak havoc on the self, spiritual, and bodily esteem of the disordered eater. In these ways, preaching becomes both a personal and political act as the whole, redeemed, affirmed body of a woman stands behind the pulpit to proclaim the Word. If this gendered proclamation espouses a theology of affirmation and liberation—one that affirms the body in all its weaknesses and disorders—it has the power to resurrect broken women's bodies into the fullness of life.

Bringing It All Together: Broken Bodies Redeemed

Does our preaching and worship acknowledge the "complexity and diversity of spiritual hungers among girls and women who are currently starving, vomiting, and choking on the symbolic beliefs and ritualizing practices that this society normally recommends to them"?[162] Entangled in the self-loathing of an eating disorder was the lack of self-worth perpetuated by the total depravity enmeshed in the faith I once claimed as my own. Through a hermeneutic of suspicion, recognition of the patriarchy that permeates the history of my religious tradition, and a feminist liberation theology, I find myself no longer in the bondage of my own guilt that I will never be good enough or skinny enough. As I have become proud of who I am as a woman, a feminist, and a lesbian, I have recognized the paradox of this issue for me. "By succumbing to cultural pressure to lose weight, I sometimes feel I've betrayed my feminist self, bought into the 'beauty myth,' failed to rebel against patriarchal standards of what women should be."[163] As I learn to deal with this tension that exists deep within my heart, I am reminded that God created *me* as a person of worth and dignity, even with my disorder. In this way, the broken body is redeemed. This is worthy of proclamation. This will preach.

Practical Applications: Sermon and Liturgy

Personal stories of disordered eating give testimony to the ways in which preachers must grapple with these difficult issues in preaching and worship. Scripture, history, and theology also provide us with the theoretical underpinnings for how such issues relate to worshipping women in today's culture. But testimony and theory are sometimes not enough. Sometimes clergy need ways to practically approach eating disorders in

---

[162] Lelwica, 146.
[163] Lelwica, 130.

worship and preaching. Accordingly, in this section I offer two practical applications. The first are a series of liturgical elements created for addressing these complex issues within the context of worship. If this is something that has never been done in your church, contacting the National Eating Disorder Association would be a good first step in finding concrete resources; perhaps choosing a Sunday that coincides with National Eating Disorder Awareness Week would provide a helpful connection with your church's contextual worshipping life. NEDAW typically occurs in early spring, which often aligns with the season of Lent. Given how fasting, soul searching, giving up temptations, and an emphasis on wilderness-times are so primary during the season of Lent, there is a natural connection in addressing the role of eating disorders and faith.

Accordingly, my second practical example is a sermon I preached during NEDAW, which fell on the first Sunday of Lent. Both the liturgy and the sermon are found on the pages that follow.

Liturgical Elements for Disordered Eaters
Hymn of Affirmation

Title: God Embodied
Tune: NICEA
Words by Angela Yarber

God embodied, God enfleshed, You breathe life into us
You have lived, have breathed, have grown inside a body
So our bodies worship you, living, breathing, growing
Bodies are our offering, for eternity

Bodies broken, bones revealed, You, our co-sufferer
When our worth and self-esteem is lost along the way
You accept our brokenness, giving healing wholeness
Bodies are our offering, for eternity

Breathe new life into us, filling all that's empty
Hungry, starving, thirsting for a love that never ends
Folds us in Your arms of love, healing all that's broken

Bodies are our offering, for eternity

Litany of Repentance and Assurance of Pardon

For the times when we fail to acknowledge our own inherent worth,
Forgive us, Creator God.
For the times when we treat our bodies as less than a holy temple, beloved, and beautiful,
Forgive us, Redeemer God.
For the times when we treat the bodies of others as anything less than fearfully and wonderfully made.
Forgive us, Sustainer God.

We know that You are our Co-Sufferer, one who knows what it is like to hurt, deny, starve.
Believe in us, we pray.
We know that Your grace is bigger than our lack of self worth and deeper than our disorders.
Believe in us, we pray.
We are confident that Your compassion pours into our emptiness so that we are filled with Your abiding love.
Believe in us, we pray.

Pastoral Prayer

To the God who Delights in Our Inmost Being,
We approach You hurt, afraid, empty, and hungry. We are hungry for a love deep enough to fill us and a grace wide enough to embrace us. We know that we are, indeed, fearfully and wonderfully made. We know that you look at us in awe, like an artist proud of a masterpiece. At the same time, we struggle. We struggle to look at our reflections. We struggle to treat our bodies as temples. We struggle to claim the worth you create in us. We struggle to eat. We struggle not purge.
So, we beg you to empower us to claim our inherent worth. Embolden us to live into the fullness of life You desire for us.

Galvanize us to eat and play and laugh and pleasure in the goodness of Your creation, which sustains and upholds and nourishes us. Never allow us to forget or forsake the bounty of the earth as it fills our bellies, nourishes our bodies, and feeds our souls. When we look into the mirror, may we see in our own bodies, a reflection of Your creative spirit stirring in us so that we are enlivened to be the presence of Christ here on earth. Feed us. Nourish us. Sustain us. Incarnate in our broken bodies, we pray. Amen.

Sermon
This sermon was preached on the first Sunday of Lent at the church I served in California. An image of Picasso's *Girl Before a Mirror* was on the cover of the worship bulletin and a poster-size print of the same painting was framed in the front of the sanctuary.

Picasso's "The Girl Before a Mirror"
National Eating Disorder Awareness Week
Luke 4:1-13

> *Jesus, full of the Holy Spirit, returned from Jordan and was led by the Spirit into the wilderness, where for forty days he was tempted by the devil. He ate nothing at all during those days, and when they were over, he was famished. The devil said to him, "If you are the Child of God, command this stone to become a loaf of bread." Jesus answered him, "It is written, 'One does not live by bread alone.'"*

Let's be honest. When we read the Lenten text about Jesus in the wilderness, the question we're all wondering is: was Jesus on the Atkins diet? "One does not live by *bread* alone." Was it the insatiable need to count carbs that led Jesus into the wilderness, escaping the temptation of sandwiches, pita pockets, tortillas, and sourdough bread bowls? Or was bathing suit season lurking just around the corner and Jesus wanted to retreat into the desert for forty days of "hot yoga," certain that the sun,

heat, and plow position, combined with utter starvation, would burn off those extra unwanted pounds?
Sacrilege! Blasphemy! Jesus didn't struggle with such things! How dare we apply our contemporary struggles, our American and privileged concerns onto the Christ, Jesus, Messiah, *Co-Sufferer*. Jesus wasn't concerned with such things…was he?

Today we enter into the season of Lent, a time when we remember Jesus' forty days in the wilderness: forty days of fasting, heat, temptation, and perhaps fear. We are focusing on the Gifts of the Wilderness in the days to come, a time when we recall our own days in the desert, what we learned there, what we needed there, and what provided strength there. Have you ever been in the wilderness? Do you recall spending time in the desert? And, no, I don't necessarily mean the literal desert or wilderness, though trading stories of camping and hiking is something I love to do. I mean those metaphorical times in the wilderness, the symbolic days in the desert. What did it feel like? Were you hungry, hot, tired, tempted, and a little afraid? What was it that gave you strength during those dry days, your symbolic stream in the metaphorical waste land? We've all had our times in the desert, and so did Jesus. Perhaps it was a time when you lost your job, or went through a divorce, or moved far away from family and friends, or watched a loved one suffer and die. These wilderness times are hard and often painful to remember. But we've all had our times in the desert.

I would like to share with you one of my wilderness times. Like your time in the desert, it was hard and often painful to remember. One of my heroes in homiletics, Barbara Brown Taylor, describes preaching as "spiritual exhibitionism," where you lay it all on the line, when you are spiritually naked in front of eager and hungry hearts. And so, at the risk of "baring it all," so to speak, will you journey with me into the wilderness? It may be hard, painful, or uncomfortable. As we journey, however, remember that we do not brave these desert roads alone; we are on this path together and have a Co-Sufferer by our sides.

Today is not only the first Sunday in Lent, but it is also the beginning of National Eating Disorder Awareness Week. Did you know that 80% of women in America struggle with a sub-clinical eating disorder? This may not be a word with which you are familiar; we hear about anorexia and bulimia and binge eating and over eating, but what's a sub-clinical eating disorder and how on earth do the majority of Americans have it? You see, a sub-clinical eating disorder is when an individual is constantly worried about food, eating, appearance, calories, exercise—when food and appearance consume one's thoughts. For me, this notion is best illustrated in Picasso's painting *Girl Before a Mirror*. I remember looking at a picture of Picasso's painting with a child. The child said that there are two girls in the picture. It's interesting that the title is *Girl*—not Girl*s*—*Before a Mirror*. One girl. One reflection. But her reflection does not really seem to mirror what she looks like, does it?

Rather, the girl, like 80 % of American women, looks into the mirror and cannot clearly see her reflection, but a distortion of it—one that is not pretty enough or skinny enough or good enough. Perhaps the girl Picasso was painting compared herself to all the models that grace the covers of magazines, or television, or movies. Perhaps the girl before Picasso's mirror looked at her reflection with tears in her hungry and wanting eyes and wondered, "Why can't I look like _______?" Maybe she was struggling with Body Dysmorphic Disorder. At one point or another we've all been Picasso's girl, Picasso's person before a mirror, where our eyes could not see our reflection clearly, but instead saw one that was less than, worse than, unworthy to see beauty reflected in the mirror. Such was the case for the majority of my adolescent years.

I'd like to share a story with you, a story that stems from one of my days in the wilderness. A story of a time when I was convinced, like Jesus, that "one does not live by bread alone." Once upon a time there was a college cheerleader named Angela. Now before you pass judgment on this chipper cheerleader, allow me to elaborate. She was not your typical cheerleader—ditsy and airhead were not a part of her vocabulary. She was actually a star student. 4.0 in the religious studies program. That's right: *religious* studies. Not only was the cheerleader a good student, but she was a youth minister at a local church, leading bible studies, mission trips, and camps for teenagers. I suppose it's safe to say that this cheerleader was not a moron, but an oxymoron. However, despite her paradoxical tendencies to defy stereotypes when it came to the brains or morals of the typical cheerleader, this college student found herself struggling with her reflection, much like Picasso's girl before a mirror. She had always been a dancer, gymnast, and performer, living her life in a leotard…surrounded by mirrors…on stage for all the world to see…every flaw visible for critique. So, maintaining weight was always an issue for the college cheerleader. In fact, she'd battled anorexia for many of her middle and high school years. But now she found herself in college: studying to make straight As, serving as a minister at the "wise" age of twenty, and battling to balance on the quivering hands of her bases that threw her tiny body into the air in cheerleading stunts. The smaller you are, the higher you fly.

So, I counted calories and exercised, aware that my 5'5" frame probably did not need to weigh so little. To make matters worse, I was a perfectionist. As a performer, my life was always on display and my new-found faith taught me to imitate Christ, to be perfect as my Heavenly Father is perfect, to deny myself, take up my cross and follow Christ. And so, I did. Perfectionism and self-loathing are recurring idioms in disorder eaters. Like the female monastics that lived hundreds of years before me, I denied myself, took up my cross and followed Christ.

In Michelle Lelwica's stirring book, *Starving for Salvation*, she quotes a young anorexic's words, "The whole life is like you are carrying a cross—something heroic, something that is very difficult and demands admiration. I felt [that] doing something that was not hard was quite inconceivable; it would be lazy and despicable." So, I took up my cross and followed a path that led only to emptiness, hurt, hunger, and a countless number of emergency room visits.

On game day, the squad was required to eat a meal before the game. "You can't cheer on an empty stomach," coach said. So, I polished off 6 Saltine crackers and a glass of water. Like, Picasso's *Girl Before a Mirror*, I stood in front my reflection, running my hands over my bony ribcage and protruding hipbones. I did not see an emaciated body staring back at me, but instead saw arms that needed toning, obliques with too much fat, and a waistline that could use some more sit-ups. I saw a hypocrite: "how can I preach to my youth group that they are made in the image of God, beautiful and beloved, and struggle so much with what I see? I am not worth the space my body takes up. Furthermore, I am succumbing to patriarchal and materialistic trends that I find oppressive. Why won't this go away? A poor girl from the projects was not made to deal with such a privileged problem. This is my choice, my disorder. Just make it go away," I thought. So, as I did after every meal, I retreated to the bathroom to hold back my hair and force my finger down my throat. When I was finished I brushed my teeth, smoothed out the pleats on my uniform, wiped the tears from my eyes, and smudged cherry-red lipstick across my mouth. As I gathered my thoughts before walking to the gym, I glanced over to my dorm room bed to see my Greek homework laying unfinished and sighed at the thought of post-game studying. I closed my notebook, and reached for my Greek New Testament. And the words of Ephesians 2:10 caught my eye.. "You are God's workmanship, God's *poema*." This word for "workmanship" in Greek is the word *poema* from which we derive our English word for poem. You are God's poem, Angela.

The college cheerleader returned to the bathroom, reopened her cherry-red lipstick and scrawled across her mirror in large letters: *poema*, promising herself and the God who created her that she would get help for her disorder. Strength in the wilderness. A stream in the desert of disorder.

You are God's workmanship. One day, God wrote a beautiful, magnificent poem and titled it Katy, Greg, Elliot, Maura, Willis, Frances. As an artist creates a masterpiece, imbuing each detail with handiwork and care and intentionality, so God has created each of you. God's fingerprints are all over you. Whether you see your reflection in the mirror and smile, or whether you look, like the *Girl Before a Mirror*, and see a distortion of that reflection, God looks at you and cries out, "If you could only see yourself through my eyes, you would marvel at the sight."

So, one does not live by bread alone…but a little bread sure does help. During this time of year, let us be mindful of those who may still find themselves in the desert. Let us remember that there are those in our world and perhaps here in this place that are struggling in the wilderness, even today. May we be a people that offer streams in dry lands. May we be a church that provides strength in the midst of heartache. If you are in a dry and hungry place, we invite you to take heart. Here is a place where you may find refuge in the wilderness. Here is a place where the living water never runs dry, no matter your situation in the desert. The road may not be easy, but it is one that we commit to taking together. And as we walk hand-in-hand along these desert pathways, let us remember that One has gone before us and walks beside us still, giving hope and peace and strength for the journey. During this season of Lent, let us be refreshing agents of hope in wilderness, a source of rest in the desert. During this week, may we be mindful of the concerns of struggling men and women around us, who look at their reflections, like Picasso's *Girl Before a Mirror*, and are unable to see the beauty with which they are created. As the One who created us and sees us wholly tells us, "you are made in my image and *that is good*." Amen.

Conclusions: When the Body Goes Awry

As we have seen, the church has often treated the body—and particularly women's bodies—as objects of shame, something to overcome, flesh in need of negation. And popular culture has taught women that bodies must look a particular way—skinny, youthful, flawless—in order to be deemed worthy. When church and popular culture collide, the lack of self-esteem in countless disordered eaters wreaks havoc on hungry bodies aching for acceptance, redemption, and salvation. This was the case in my personal struggle with disordered eating. It was the case in the history of the Christian church and in many artistic depictions of a crucified Jesus. And it continues to be the case for countless women who fill the pews each Sunday, even for many whose broken bodies stand behind the pulpit.

In order for our preaching and worship to be responsible, it is our duty to name, acknowledge, and feed our starving sisters. By preaching as testimony and admonishing sacramental permeability at the shared meal we are emboldened to be and become prophetic voices—prophetic bodies—that struggle, ache, grow, and desire together. In these ways, our sermons, our presiding with the bread and the cup, our songs, our liturgies, our very bodies before the congregation gender the pulpit and worship space. This gendering is a redemptive act that acknowledges that all bodies are in need of resurrection, hope, and healing. We are the body of Christ, after all, and sometimes the body of Christ is disordered. For our preaching and worship to deny or hide this, we deny and hide part of Christ's body here on earth.

Chapter 8
Conclusions: Gendering the Pulpit in the Direction of Justice

RAGING, AGING, SUFFERING, STARVING BODIES stand behind the pulpit. Dancing, affirmed, honored, celebrated bodies stand behind the pulpit. Sexualized, queer, subversive, transgressive bodies stand behind the pulpit. Gendered, essentialized, constructed, oppressed bodies stand behind the pulpit. We are the Body of Christ—gendered, sexualized, dancing, and disordered—and our bodies preach on our behalf before we utter a word. Our bodies proclaim the Word. Our genders proclaim the Word. Our sexuality proclaims the Word. And when we proclaim these Words, we gender the pulpit in the direction of justice, inclusion, and radical hospitality.

In the same way that queer theorists claim that our gendered and sexualized bodies are constructed by society, I would like to claim that our bodies construct the sermon and the pulpit constructs our bodies. Gendering the pulpit in the direction of justice means that the preacher has a choice. The preacher can dismantle the status quo or maintain it. The preacher can uphold patriarchal norms or overturn them. The preacher can subvert heteronormative oppression or condone it. As I have shown throughout this book, it is not the preacher's disembodied voice alone that can gender the pulpit. It takes the preacher's entire body. When the preacher permits the entire gendered and sexualized body to infiltrate the pulpit, the sermon is constructed in the direction of redemption and resurrection. If Jesus felt that the body was important enough to be resurrected, then the body is important enough to proclaim resurrection from the pulpit.

It has been my aim in this book to suggest how one might gender the pulpit by exploring sex, body, and desire. Personal narratives, theory, and praxis have combined to offer glimpses into the roles of gender, sexuality, dance, and disorder in gendering the pulpit. With scripture, history, theology, theories or preaching and worship, and practical examples now firmly in our grasp, I close with a story of how we all hold the potential for resurrection in our bodies—our gendered, sexualized, dancing, and disordered bodies—and how these very bodies have the power to gender the pulpit.

During my last semester in seminary I attended our weekly chapel service. Singing, praying, preaching, communion: there was nothing unusual about worship. In fact, I don't remember who preached, what songs we sang, or who was lifted up during the prayers of the people. As worship was coming to a close, I noticed something printed in the bulletin that was cause for concern: the Apostle's Creed. Reciting the Apostle's Creed was not a normative part of our worshipping life at my seminary. It was a Baptist seminary, after all, and Baptists aren't creedal. Plus, seminary is typically a time of great cynicism, cognitive dissonance, a time when heresy is permitted and questions abound. I couldn't image many of my classmates—myself included—affirming all the words in the creed.

The time came for us all to recite the creed, neatly printed in our bulletins. I sighed an exasperated sigh, rolled my eyes, and mumbled along, aware that a sense of community was probably more important that my own theological disbelief. Bodies standing, hands gripping crumpled bulletins, voices united, we all proclaimed, "I believe in God..." As the creed continued, everyone listed the things we believe: "communion of saints, forgiveness of sins, etc." I continued to mumble. But when we reached the phrase "the resurrection of the body" something happened. "I believe in the resurrection of the body." If I'm honest, I don't really believe that, at least not in the traditional sense. But in community I recited those words and surprised myself as tears began to fill my eyes.

You see, I might not believe in the resurrection of a literal body. I believe that Jesus' body is resurrected in each of us, in our bodies. We are the resurrected body of Christ. We embody resurrection when we live into all the things I've discussed in this book. We proclaim the bodily resurrection when the gendered, sexualized, dancing, disordered body is affirmed and celebrated. When we create places for all marginalized bodies—gendered, racialized, sexualized bodies—to have opportunities for resurrection: that is the resurrection of the body. If we do not create these pathways to resurrection for all humanity, I am convinced that Jesus' body remains in the tomb. It is our actions, our inactions, that keep Jesus tethered to the grave. It is our actions, our bodies, our proclamations that create resurrection.

In that moment, when I recited that line in the Apostle's Creed, I realized that I actually can believe in the resurrection of the body. It was as though the creed was telling me, "There's hope for your body yet, Angela." My disordered, dancing, gendered, sexualized, queer body was experiencing resurrection. In that moment, in the recitation of that creed, I realized my calling and responsibility to gender the pulpit. For when our bodies gender the pulpit, we all have the opportunity to experience the resurrection of the body. When we gender the pulpit in the direction of justice, there is enough resurrection for every body.

Bibliography

Adams, Doug. *Eyes to See Wholeness: Visual Arts Informing Biblical and Theological Studies in Education and Worship Through the Church Year*. Prescott: EMI, 1995.

__________, and Diane Apostolos-Cappadona, ed. *Art as Religious Studies*. New York: Crossroads Publishing, 1987.

__________. *Dance as Religious Studies*. New York: Crossroads Publishing, 1990.

Alcoff, Linda. "Cultural Feminism versus Post-Structuralism: The Identity Crisis in Feminist Theory." In *Feminist Theory: A Reader*, 426-436, ed. Wendy Kolmar and Frances Bartkowski. New York: McGraw Hill, 2005.

Althaus-Reid, Marcella. I*ndecent Theology*. London: SCM Press, 1997.

Apostolos-Cappadona, Diann, ed. *Art, Creativity, and the Sacred*. New York: Continuum, 1995.

Barger, Lilian. *Eve's Revenge: Women and A Spirituality of the Body*. Grand Rapids: Brazos Press, 2003.

Bailey,Derrick. *Homosexuality and the Western Christian Tradition*. London: Longmans, Green, 1955.

Beiler, Andrea, and Luisa Schonoff. *The Eucharist: Bodies, Bread, and Resurrection*. Minneapolis: Fortress Press, 2007.

Bringle, Mary Louise. "Swallowing the Shame: Pastoral Care Issues in Food Abuse." *Journal of Pastoral Care* 48.2 (Summer, 1994): 135-144.

Boswell, John. *Christianity, Social Tolerance, and Homosexuality.* Chicago: Chicago University Press, 1980.

Brock, Rita. "The Feminist Redemption of Christ," In *Christian Feminism: Visions of a New Humanity*, ed. Judith Weidman. New York: Harper and Row, 1984.

Brown, Teresa Fry. *Delivering the Sermon*. Minneapolis: Fortress Press, 2008.

__________. *Weary Throats and New Songs*. Nashville: Abingdon Press, 2003.

Butler, Judith. *Bodies that Matter*. New York: Routledge, 1993.

__________. *Gender Trouble: Feminism and the Subversion of Identity*. New York: Routledge, 1990.

__________. "Performative Acts and Gender Constitution: An Essay in Phenomenology and Feminist Theory," *Theatre Journal* 49:1 (December 1988).

__________. *The Psychic Life of Power.* Palo Alto: Stanford University Press, 1997.

Cheng, Patrick. *From Sin to Amazing Grace.* New York: Seabury Books, 2012.

__________. *Radical Love.* New York: Seabury Books, 2011.

Cherry, Kittredge and Sherwood Zalmon. *Equal Rites: Lesbian and Gay Worship, Ceremonies, and Celebrations.* Louisville: Westminster/John Knox Press, 1995.

Childers, Jana, ed. *Birthing the Sermon*. St. Louis: Chalice Press, 2001.

__________. *Performing the Word*. Nashville: Abingdon, 1998.

Clader, Linda. *Voicing the Vision*. Harrisburg: Morehouse Publishing, 2003.

Clark, Michael. *A Place to Start.* Dallas: Monument Press, 1989.

Clarkson, Shanon. "Inclusive Language and the Church." *Prism: A Theological Forum for the UCC* 5:2 (Fall 1990): 37-49.

Cleaver, Richard. *Know My Name: A Gay Liberation Theology.* Louisville: Westminster John Knox, 1995.

Coulton, Nicolas, Ed. *The Bible, the Church, and Homosexuality.* London: Darton, Longman and Todd, 2005.

Cousar, Charles. *The Letters of Paul*. Nashville: Abingdon Press, 1996.

Daly, Mary. *The Church and the Second Sex.* Boston: Beacon Press, 1968.

DeConick, April. *Holy Misogyny.* New York: Continuum, 2011.

DeSola, Carla. "Liturgical Dance: State of the Art." In *Postmodern Worship and the Arts*, ed. Doug Adams and Michael Moynahan. San Jose: Resource Publications, 2002.

Douglas, Kelly Brown. *The Black Christ*. Maryknoll: Orbis Books, 1994.

__________ and Marvin Ellison, Eds. *Sexuality and the Sacred*. Louisville: Westminster John Knox Press, 2010.

Drinkwater, Greg, Joshua Lesser, and David Shneer. *Torah Queeries.* New York: New York University Press, 2009.

"Eating Disorders." *Diagnostic and Statistical Manual of Mental Disorder –IV –TR*, 4th ed. Washington D.C.: American Psychiatric Association, 2000.

Edwards, George. *Gay/Lesbian Liberation.* New York: Pilgrim Press, 1984.

Elliott, Clifford. "Crucified Woman." *International Review of Mission* 71(Winter 1982): 332-35.

Feder, Bernard and Elaine. *The Expressive Arts Therapies*. New Jersey: Prentice-Hall, Inc., 1981.

Fennema, Sharon. "Falling All Around Me: Worship Performing Theodicy in the Midst of the San Francisco AIDS Crisis." Ph.D. Dissertation, Graduate Theological Union, 2011.

Fletcher, Karen Baker. *Dancing with God.* St. Louis: Chalice Press, 2006.

Florence, Anna Carter. *Preaching as Testimony*. Louisville: Westminster John Knox, 2007.

Floyd, Samuel. "Ring Shout! Literary Studies, Historical Studies, and Black Music Inquiry." *Black Music Research Journal,* Vol. 22 (2002).

Forman, Kristen, ed. *The New Century Hymnal Companion*. Cleveland: The Pilgrim Press, 1998.

Gagne, Ronald, Thomas Kane, and Robert VerEecke, *Introducing Dance in Christian Worship* Portland: Pastoral Press, 1999.

Garrigan, Siobhan. "Queer Worship." *Theology and Sexuality* 15: 2 (May 2009): 211-30.

Gomes, Peter. *The Good Book.* San Francisco: HarperSanFrancisco, 1996.

Gomez, Michael. *Exchanging Our Country Masks.* Chapel Hill: University of North Carolina Press, 1998.

Grant, Jacquelyn. *White Women's Christ and Black Women's Jesus.* Atlanta: Scholars Press, 1989.

Griffith, Marie. *Born Again Bodies*. Berkeley: University of California Press, 2004.

Gruber, Mayer. "Ten Dance-Derived Expressions in the Hebrew Bible." In *Dance as Religious Studies*, ed. Doug Adams and Diane Apostolos-Cappadona, 48-66. New York: Crossroads Publishing Company, 1990).

Guest, Deryn, Robert Goss, Mona West, and Thomas Bohache, Eds. *The Queer Bible Commentary.* London: SCM Press, 2006.

Hall, Douglas. *The Cross in Our Context*. Minneapolis: Fortress Press, 2003.

Harris, Stephen. *The New Testament*. Mountain View: Mayfield Publishing Company, 1999.

Heller, Ena, ed. *Reluctant Partners: Art and Religion in Dialogue*. New York: Gallery of the American Bible Society, 2004.

Helminiak, Daniel. *What the Bible Really Says about Homosexuality.* San Francisco: Alamo Square Press, 1994.

Heyward, Carter. *Touching Our Strength: The Erotic as Power and the Love of God.* New York: HarperSanFrancisco, 1989.

Hinkle, Don. "CBF homosexuality stance ignites controversy over group's direction." *Baptist Press* (October 27, 2000), http://baptist2baptist.net/printfriendly.asp?ID=187 [accessed January 18, 2013].

Hinnant, Olive. *God Comes Out: A Queer Homiletic.* Cleveland: Pilgrim Press, 2007.

Horsleu, G.H.R. *New Documents Illustrating Early Christianity*. Ancient History Documentary Research Centre: Macquarie University, 1981.

Hunt, Mary. *Fierce Tenderness.* New York: Crossroad, 1991.

Jakobsen, Janet and Ann Pellegrini. *Love the Sin: Sexual Regulation and the Limits of Religious Tolerance.* New York: New York University Press, 2003.

James, Rob and Gary Leazer. *The Fundamentalist Takeover in the Southern Baptist Convention* Timiosoara: Impact Media, 1999.

Jensen, Robin. "The Suffering and Dead Christ in Early Christian Art." *ARTS* (August 2001):22-28.

Johnson, Elizabeth. *She Who Is.* New York: Crossroad, 1992.

Kuster, Volker. *The Many Faces of Jesus Christ.* Maryknoll: Orbis Books, 1999.

Lelwica, Michelle Mary. *Starving for Salvation: The Spiritual Dimensions of Eating Problems Among American Girls and Women.* New York: Oxford University Press, 1998.

Levine, Lawrence. *Black Culture and Black Consciousness.* Oxford: Oxford University Press, 1977.

Linn, Dennis, Sheila, and Matthew. *Good Goats: Healing Our Image of God.* New York: Paulist Press, 1986.

Loughlin, Gerard, Ed. *Queer Theology*. Malden: Blackwell, 2007.

Maine, Margo. *Body Wars: Making Peace with Women's Bodies.* Carlsbad: Gurze Books, 2000.

_________. *Father Hunger: Fathers, Daughters and Food.* Carlsbad: Gurze Books, 1991.

Marshall, Paul. *Same-Sex Unions: Stories and Rites.* New York: Church Publishing, 2004.

Migliore, Daniel. *Faith Seeking Understanding: An Introduction to Christian Theology*. Grand Rapids: William B. Eerdmans Publishing Company, 1991.

Moltmann-Wendel, Elizabeth. *I Am My Body: A Theology of Embodiment*. New York: Continuum, 1995.

Morrison, Toni. *Beloved.* New York: Penguin Group, 1987.

Norris, Kathleen. "Advent." In *Imaging the Liturgical Year*, eds. Susan Blain, Sharon Iverson Gouwens, Catherine 'Callaghan, and Grant Spradling. Vol. 3. Cleveland: United Church Press, 1996.

Northrup, Chrstiane. *Women's Bodies, Women's Wisdom*. New York: Bantam Books, 1987.

Orbach, Susie. *Fat is a Feminist Issue*. Berkeley: Berkeley Publishing Corporation, 1978.

Petroff, Elizabeth Alvilda. *Body and Soul: Essays on Medieval Women and Mysticism*. New York: Oxford University Press, 1994.

Plank, Karl. "Broken Continuities: *Night* and W*hite Crucifixion*." *The Christian Century* 104 (November 1987): 963-66.

Plate, Brent, ed. *Religion, Art, and Visual Culture: A Cross-Cultural Reader*. New York: Palgrave, 2002.

Polinska, Wioletta. "Bodies Under Siege: Eating Disorders and Self-Mutilation among Women." *Journal of the American Academy of Religion* 68.3 (September 2000): 569-89.

Procter-Smith, Marjorie. *In Her Own Rite: Constructing Feminist Liturgical Tradition* Nashville: Abingdon,1990.

Raboteau, Albert. *Slave Religion: The "Invisible Institution" in the Antebellum South.* New York: Oxford University Press, 1978.

Ramshaw, Gail. *Liturgical Language.* Collegeville: Liturgical Press, 1996.

Rich, Adrienne. *On Lies, Secrets, and Silence.* New York: Norton, 1979.

Rock, Judith. *Terpsichore at Louis-le-Grand: Baroque Dance on the Jesuit Stage in Paris.* Saint Louis: The Institute of Jesuit Sources, 1996.

__________ and Norman Mealy, *Performer as Priest and Prophet.* San Francisco: Harper and Row Publishers, 1988.

Rosenbaum, Art. *Shout Because You're Free: The African American Ring Shout Tradition in Coastal Georgia.* Athens: University of Georgia Press, 1998.

Ruether, Rosemary. *To Change the World: Christology and Cultural Criticism.* New York:Crossroads Publishing,1981.

Russell, Letty. *Human Liberation in a Feminist Perspective.* Philadelphia:The Westminster Press, 1974.

Schneir, Miriam. *Feminism: The Essential Historical Writings.* New York: Vintage Books, 1972.

Schreiter, Robert, ed. *Faces of Jesus in Africa.* Maryknoll: Orbis Books, 1991.

Shaw, Teresa. *The Burden of the Flesh: Fasting and Sexuality in Early Christianity*. Minneapolis: Fortress Press, 1998.

Shepherd, M. "Christology: A Central Problem of Early Christian Theology and Art." In *Age of Spirituality: A Symposium*, ed. K. Weitzmann, 108-19. New York: Norton, 1980.

Sherman, Cecil. "About Homosexuality." *Baptist Today* (April 1, 1994).

Shoop, Marcia Mount. *Let the Bones Dance.* Louisville: Westminster John Knox, 2010.

Siker, Jeffery. *Homosexuality in the Church.* Louisville: Westminster John Knox, 1994.

Smith, Christine. *Preaching as Weeping, Confession, and Resistance.* Louisville: Westminster John Knox Press, 1992.

Steensma, Regnerus. "The Image of Christ in Contemporary British Art." *ARTS* (December 2001):30-38.

Stewart, Iris. *Sacred Woman Sacred Dance*. Rochester: Inner Traditions, 2000.

Stein, Robert. *Jesus the Messiah*. Downers Grove: Intervarsity Press, 1996.

Stroup, Karen. "God Our Mother: A Call to Truly Inclusive Language." *Lexington Theological Quarterly* 27 (January 1992): 12-13.

Stuart, Elizabeth, Ed. *Daring to Speak Love's Name: A Gay and Lesbian Prayer Book.* London: Hamish Hamilton, 1992.

__________. *Just Good Friends.* London: Mowbray, 1995.

Sugirtharajah, R.S., ed. *Asian Faces of Jesus*. Maryknoll: Orbis Books, 1993.

Syndicus, E. *Early Christian Art*. Translated by J.R. Foster. New York: Hawthorn, 1962.

The Baptist Faith and Message. Nashville: LifeWay Christian Resources, 2000.

Thangaraj, Thomas. *The Crucified Guru: An Experiment in Cross-Cultural Christology*. Nashville: Abingdon Press, 1994.

Tinsley, E.J. "The Coming of a Dead and Naked Christ." *Religion* 2 (1972): 24-36.

Trull, Audra and Joe Trull, eds. *Putting Women in Their Place*. Macon: Smyth and Helwys, 2003.

Turner, Mary Donovan and Mary Lin Hudson. *Saved from Silence*. St. Louis: Chalice Press, 1999.

Van Der Leeuw, Gerardus. *Sacred and Profane Beauty: The Holy in Art*. Translated by David Green. New York: Holt, Rinehart, and Winston, Inc., 1963.

Vrudny, Kimberly, and Wilson Yates, ed. *Arts, Theology, and the Church: New Intersections*. Cleveland: Pilgrim Press, 2005.

Walker, Alice. *In Search of our Mothers' Gardens: Womanist Prose*. New York: Harcourt, 1983.

Walton, Janet. *Worship and the Arts: A Vital Connection*. Collegeville: The Liturgical Press, 1988.

Warner, Sharon. "The Value of Particularity: Inclusive Language Revisited." *Lexington:Theological Quarterly 29:4* (Winter 1994): 249-260.

Ward, Richard. *Speaking of the Holy.* St. Louis: Chalice Press, 2001.

Weaver, Aaron. "Progressive Baptist Dissenters: A History of the Alliance of Baptists," http://www.allianceofbaptists.org/learn/about/history [accessed January 15, 2013].

Weidman, Judith, ed. *Christian Feminism.* New York: Harper and Row, 1984.

Write, N.T. *Jesus and the Victory of God.* Minneapolis: Fortress Press, 1996.

Yarber, Angela. *Dance in Scripture: How Biblical Dancers Can Revolutionize Worship Today* Eugene: Wipf and Stock, 2013 forthcoming.

CPSIA information can be obtained at www.ICGtesting.com
Printed in the USA
BVOW012028120613

323107BV00010B/488/P